GREAT
CROSS-STITCH
PROJECTS AND
PATTERNS

GREAT CROSS-STITCH

PROJECTS AND PATTERNS

SEDGEWOOD™ PRESS

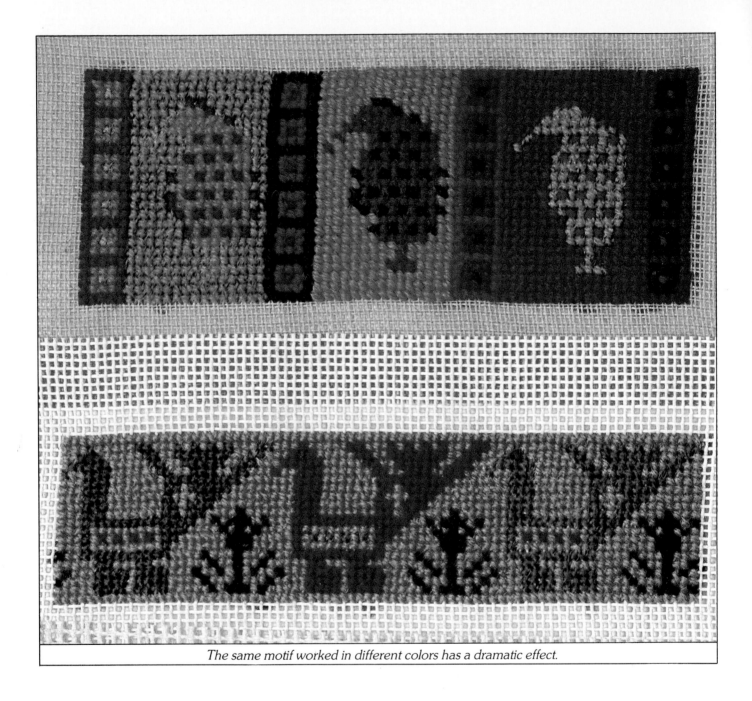

The same motif worked in different colors has a dramatic effect.

Published by Sedgewood™ Press

For Sedgewood™ Press
Editorial Director: Jane Ross
Managing Editor: Gale Kremer
Production Manager: Bill Rose

Produced for Sedgewood™ Press by
Marshall Cavendish Books
58 Old Compton Street
London W1V 5PA

For Marshall Cavendish
Editor: Maggi McCormick
Art Director: Brenda Morrison
Designer: Liz Rose
Production Manager: Dennis Hovell

First printing
© 1984 Marshall Cavendish Limited
Distributed in the Trade by
Van Nostrand Reinhold
ISBN 0-442-28203-6
Library of Congress Catalog Number
83-51237
Manufactured in the
United States of America

CONTENTS

THE
BASICS OF
CROSS-STITCH

It's easy to see why cross-stitch is one of the most popular of all embroidery stitches. Easy to work, suitable for household linens, clothing and purely decorative objects, it also lends itself readily to both naturalistic and stylized designs. For centuries it has been used to decorate peasant costume, particularly in Eastern Europe. Traditionally it has been worked in bright colors on white fabric, often in intricate designs producing a rich effect. Its angularity makes it equally suited to charming, naive motifs, such as the little flowers, animals and human figures found in the cross-stitch samplers worked by young girls in the 19th century, which also featured numerals, alphabets and inspirational mottoes.

Today cross-stitch is used for a great variety of work, from delicately-shaded pictures of wild flowers to hard-wearing rugs in bold, geometric designs. It is one of the most frequently-used needlepoint stitches, being almost as small-scale as tent stitch and nearly as durable. It combines easily with other embroidery stitches, particularly with others that involve the counting of background threads. A notable example is Assisi work, in which cross-stitch is used to fill the spaces around the motifs (left blank) and Holbein stitch is used for outlines and detail.

Fabrics and threads
The effectiveness of cross-stitch depends to a great extent on its regularity: all the stitches should be the same size and exactly square. For this reason it should, preferably, be worked on a fabric having the same number of threads vertically and horizontally. Needlepoint canvas and rug canvas obviously fall into this category. For clothing, household linens and other soft items, the best fabric is an evenweave linen or cotton on which the threads can easily be counted. Single evenweave comes in a wide range of weights, having between 14 and 36 threads to the inch, and in a variety of colors. Hardanger is a similar fabric with a double thread weave. Aida cloth, woven in multiples of threads for a basketweave effect, is another popular fabric for cross-stitch.

It is also possible to work cross-stitch on fabric with an uneven weave or too fine a weave to permit threads to be counted. A small-check gingham lends itself readily to cross-stitch, for each stitch can be worked over one square. A solid-color fabric can be used with hot-iron transfer designs, but this may not produce such good results, owing to slight irregularities in the printing. A more satisfactory method is to work the stitches over a layer of needlepoint canvas, which is later removed, thread by thread.

To work over canvas Choose a canvas with a gauge that will produce a stitch of the desired size. Either mono or double-thread (Penelope) canvas can be used, but avoid the interlock type of mono, which cannot be un-woven. Baste the canvas to the fabric, making sure that the fabric is lying smooth, with its grain aligned with the canvas threads. Work the embroidery as usual. When the embroidery is complete, dampen the work thoroughly by laying a wet towel on top of it for a few moments. Then gently pull out the dampened canvas threads (see page 76 for further information).

Many kinds of threads and yarn can be used for cross-stitch, from rug yarn down to a single strand of embroidery floss. Obviously, the thickness of the thread should be in proportion to the weight of the fabric. If you are working on needlepoint canvas, make sure that the thread covers the canvas adequately; Persian and crewel yarn can be used on a wide range of

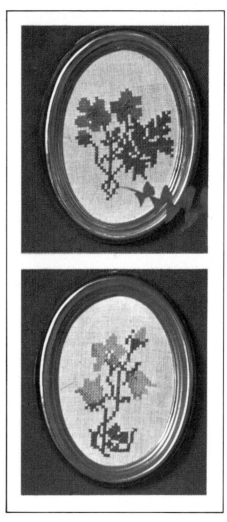

Two simple treatments of the same flower design

7

canvases by varying the number of strands used. Tapestry wool is more limited and is best suited to No. 14 canvas.

When working on evenweave fabric, you should choose a thread more or less equal in weight to the fabric threads. Stranded embroidery floss is the most versatile in this respect, as you can use from one to six strands, as appropriate. Its silky texture gives an attractive sheen to the stitches. For medium to coarse evenweave you can also use pearl cotton, No. 5 or 8, or *coton à broder,* which also give a lustrous effect. For a dull finish, choose matte embroidery cotton.

A tapestry needle is the type generally used for cross-stitch; its blunt end slips easily between the fabric threads without splitting them. If, however, the fabric is very closely woven, a sharp-pointed crewel needle can be used.

Frames and hoops

A frame is not usually necessary when working cross-stitch on canvas, for this stitch doesn't distort the canvas badly, particularly if it is worked with an easy, relaxed tension. When working on soft fabric, however, you may find a frame helpful. It holds the fabric taut, keeping the threads at right angles and making them easier to count. It also helps you to work with an even tension. A hoop is perfectly satisfactory for most cross-stitch projects. Mount the fabric in the frame by first placing it, right side up, over the inner ring, then pressing the outer ring down over the fabric, having first adjusted the outer ring so that it will grip the fabric snugly. Don't try to adjust the ring after it is in place; remove it, re-adjust and try again. The fabric should be as taut as the surface of a drum.

If you are working the design on clothing and using a frame, make sure before cutting out the pattern pieces that you have enough fabric around the design to fit the frame. If not, baste around the pattern outlines, position the design and work the embroidery; then trim away the excess fabric. You can dispense with a frame if you are working the design over canvas, for this keeps the fabric reasonably flat and regulates the stitches.

Working cross-stitch

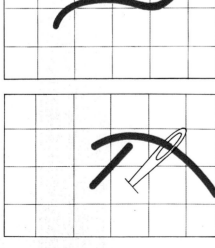

Working the stitches

Cross-stitch consists of two diagonal stitches forming an "x." To work an individual stitch: (1) Bring the needle up at the lower right-hand corner and take it down at the upper left-hand corner, crossing the same number of vertical and horizontal threads. (2) Bring the needle out at the lower left-hand corner and take it down at the upper right. It can, instead, be worked with the upper stitch sloping upward from right to left, but all stitches within the piece of work must slope the same way. A stitch worked in the opposite direction will catch the light differently and spoil the effect. If you are working lines or blocks of stitches in the same color, it's best to work in rows, completing step 1 of all the stitches, then working back in the opposite direction to complete the crosses. This method has the advantage of ensuring that all the stitches slant the same way, and it also helps you to maintain an even tension. Whether you are working stitches individually or in rows, make sure that adjacent stitches are worked into the same holes. Unless the fabric is sheer, it is permissible to carry the thread across the back of the work for short distances.

Working and adapting a design

Designs for cross-stitch embroidery are normally given in chart form, with each square representing one stitch. Charts for multicolored designs may use matching colors or may represent the colors with matching symbols. Instructions generally specify the recommended thread count for the background fabric and the number of threads to be covered by each stitch, but you can adjust the size by using a finer or coarser fabric or by working over a different number of threads. In this case, you should also use a different weight of thread. Make a small sample using a substitute fabric and thread to see how the two work together.

You can also enlarge a design by working more than one stitch for each square on the chart. By working four stitches for each square you double the size of the design; by working nine stitches for each one, you make it three times as large. In this way you could, for example, take a design intended for a pincushion and use it for a pillow cover. If you are altering the design in this way, it is best to make a new chart on graph paper, substituting the new multiple of squares for each square on the original— trying to enlarge as you stitch is risky.

You can adapt cross-stitch designs in many other ways. For example, you could take a design intended to be worked in a dark color on white fabric and reverse it by working it in white or cream on a dark fabric. You could take a single motif from a picture and repeat it around the hem of a skirt or on a belt. Or take a single letter from a sampler alphabet and use it for a monogrammed needlepoint pillow, working it in different sizes and colors in a scattered effect. A tent stitch needlepoint design can be worked in cross-stitch on canvas, leaving the background in tent stitch, or on even-weave fabric to make a tablecloth. The possibilities are endless.

Pressing and blocking

Before a completed piece of embroidery can be framed, or incorporated into a finished garment or accessory, it must be pressed or blocked to remove any wrinkles or distortion of the fabric. If the work has become soiled, it may also need washing or cleaning. Either hand-wash it gently or take it to a good dry cleaner.

Cross-stitch worked in rows

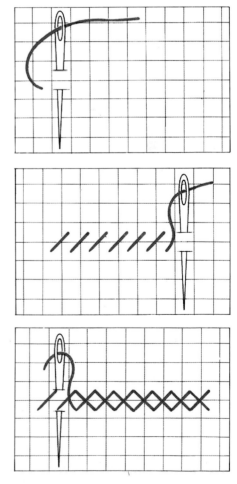

9

Normally a piece of cross-stitch embroidery worked on evenweave or another soft fabric requires only pressing. Press it face down over a folded turkish towel, using a damp press cloth.

In some cases—such as a panel worked on heavy fabric—it may be necessary to block the work in order to remove the wrinkles entirely and correct any distortion that may have occurred. For this you need a softwood board, about ½ inch thick and at least a few inches larger than the fabric, a piece of muslin or an old sheet slightly larger than the board, thumbtacks or a staple gun, carpet tacks, a hammer and a right-angled triangle.

Cover the board with the muslin, pulling it smooth and fastening the edges to the wrong side with thumbtacks or staples. Soak the embroidery in cold water. Lay it on the covered board, right side down—unless it includes raised stitches, in which case it should be right side up. Nail the four corners to the board, making sure (with the triangle) that they form 90° angles and that the fabric is taut. Then place a carpet tack in the center of each side. Continue tacking around the edges until the tacks are about ½ inch apart. Allow the work to dry thoroughly.

The procedure for blocking needlepoint is slightly different. Instead of muslin, a piece of blotting paper is used to cover the surface of the board. On the paper, draw the outline of the finished work, using pencil or indelible pen, a ruler and a right-angled triangle. Draw a line through the vertical and horizontal centers of the shape. Tape or tack the paper to the board. Prepare the canvas by marking the center of each side (if you have not already done so) and removing the masking tape and selvage, if any, from the edges. Dampen the work by steam pressing, if it is only slightly distorted, or saturating it with a wet sponge. Place it on the marked outline and nail it down, starting at the center marks, then continuing along the sides, nailing down first one pair of opposite sides and then the other, so that the edges fit the outline exactly. Allow the work to dry thoroughly.

Mounting embroidery for framing

An embroidered picture must be mounted on a piece of cardboard before framing, so as to keep its surface smooth. For this you will need a piece of cardboard about ⅛ inch thick, some strong thread, such as button thread, and a large needle. The cardboard should be slightly larger than the picture area to allow for the overlapping edge of the frame or mat. If desired, a thin layer of batting can be glued to one side of the cardboard; this gives an extra-smooth, padded surface.

Place the embroidery face up on the cardboard, making sure that it is aligned correctly, with an even margin all around. Insert a few straight pins in the edges to hold the fabric in place temporarily, and turn the work over. Fold the two longer sides over the cardboard edges. Using a long single strand of thread, knotted at the end, lace the two edges together. Start at the middle and work all the way to one edge of the cardboard, placing the stitches about ½- to ¾-inch apart; then work from the middle to the other edge. Fasten the thread securely at each end. Then fold the shorter sides over (there is no need to miter the corners) and lace them together. The embroidery is now ready for framing. (See page 146 for more information.)

Making a pillow cover

To make a pillow you will need a piece of backing fabric in a color har-

monizing with the embroidery and a pillow form 1 inch larger in both directions than the embroidered piece; this will ensure a good, plump shape. If you are cording the edges, you will need filler cord and enough extra backing fabric to cover it with bias strips.

Mark the finished edge of the embroidery—the seamline—with a marking pen and ruler on the wrong side of the fabric. Trim the seam allowance to ¾ inch. Cut a piece of backing fabric the same size. If you are cording the edges, prepare the cording as described below and baste it to the right side of the embroidered piece, with the cord inward and the raw edges match-

A selection of the threads, needles and fabrics available for working cross-stitch.

A landscape picture worked in cross-stitch.

ing. Overlap the ends of the cording by 1 inch. Unpick the stitches on one end for a little more than an inch and pull back the fabric. Trim the cord so that it meets the other end exactly. Smooth the fabric over the joining, turning under the raw edge. Hand-sew the fabric strip in place again. Clip the cording seam allowances around curves.

Place the backing piece over the embroidered piece with right sides facing. Baste around all four edges. Stitch along the seamline with the embroidered piece upward, following the marked line and using the cording foot if the edge is being corded. Leave an opening in one side—8 inches is adequate for most pillow covers. If the cover is made of needlepoint, make sure that the seams are right up against the embroidery; otherwise canvas threads will show at the edges.

Trim the seam allowances to different depths (called "grading"), tapering them close to the stitching at the corners. Turn the cover right side out. Insert the pillow form. Turn in the edges of the opening and slip stitch them together.

To make cording: Cut one or more strips of the backing fabric on the true bias—that is, at a 45° angle to the selvage. To determine the width of the strips, measure the circumference of the filler cord and add twice the pillow cover's seam allowance. Join strips, if necessary, to make up the length to go around the pillow, seaming them on the straight grain of the fabric. Fold the bias strip around the filler cord, right side out. Using the cording or zipper foot of the machine, stitch close to the cord along its entire length.

PILLOWS
AND
PICTURES

Down on the farm

This charming Alpine farmyard scene has the potential to be anything from a picture for a child's room to decoration on a sweater.

Size
14 x 24in

You will need
½yd of 24in-wide evenweave linen
1 skein of stranded embroidery floss in each of the following colors: black, brown, tan, beige, orange, yellow, red, green, navy blue and medium blue
Tapestry needle
Button thread
Cardboard for mounting

To work the embroidery
Using 2 strands of embroidery floss, work as shown in the photograph and charts. Work each stitch over 2 threads of fabric.

Use your personal taste and imagination to alter the colors and facial expressions of the animals. Attention paid to such details will enliven all your efforts. For example, the cows are all standing in slightly different positions and have their tails held in different ways. Notice how spaces between stitches are used to suggest features.

If you do not wish to make a complete garment from evenweave fabric, work the embroidery and cut around the motif, leaving a margin of about 1in to apply as a bound hem to the finished item.

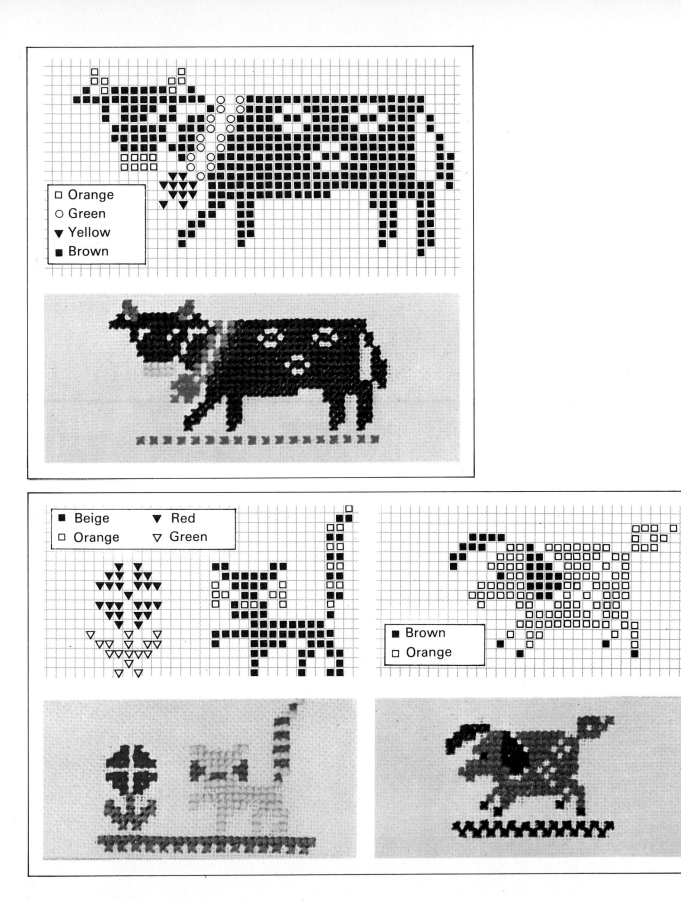

Fancy footwork

This charming anemone design dresses up a footstool. Make a matching pillow for extra comfort.

Size
Stool 11½ x 17in

You will need
Mono canvas with 20 threads to 1in (see below for a guide to measuring)
Crewel yarn in the following colors and quantities: 12 skeins of dark olive; 8 skeins of white; 2 skeins of light olive; 3 skeins of medium olive; 1 skein of pale lime
Tapestry needle

Anemone Footstool and Pillow
For a footstool with a side drop, extend the background to the size desired. Leave the corner areas unworked.
Mark the center lines of the canvas. Count and mark the extent of the chart with lines of basting. Each square represents one stitch. Using 2 strands of thread, begin at one side and work across the chart, completing each row of pattern and background. Work over 2 threads. Add textural interest by working larger cross-stitches over four threads at the center of the flower. Stretch and finish the stool as shown below.
The pillow is shown with the design repeated twice, or you can use the design exactly as shown on the footstool.

Special technique — Making a stool

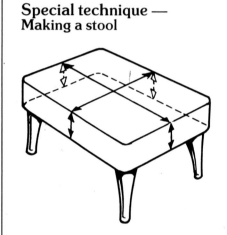

1. *Measure the length, width and depth of the top of the stool. Add 6 inches to each measurement to allow for stretching and finishing.*

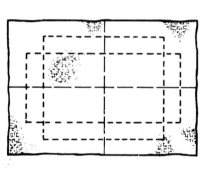

2. *Mark the center, both lengthwise and widthwise, of the canvas with basting. Then mark the outlines of the stool with basting, extending each side to include the depth of the side drop. Work the embroidery inside these lines.*

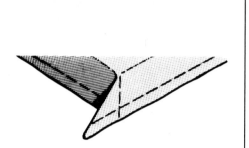

3. *When the embroidery is completed, stretch the finished embroidery. Bring the corners together, right sides facing, and stitch them close to the embroidery. Trim the seam allowance on the bottom edge to 1½in.*

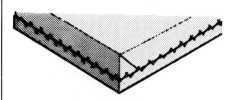

4. *Fold the corner triangles to one side and turn up the hem allowance. Herringbone-stitch in place on the wrong side, catching in the corner triangles as you work. Turn the cover right side out.*

5. *Fit the cover over the stool. Working from the center of each side in turn, secure the cover with upholstery tacks. Smooth the canvas as you work. Cover the tacks with co-ordinating braid if you wish.*

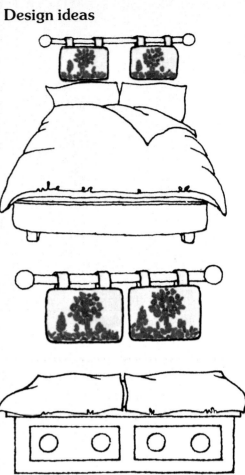

Design ideas

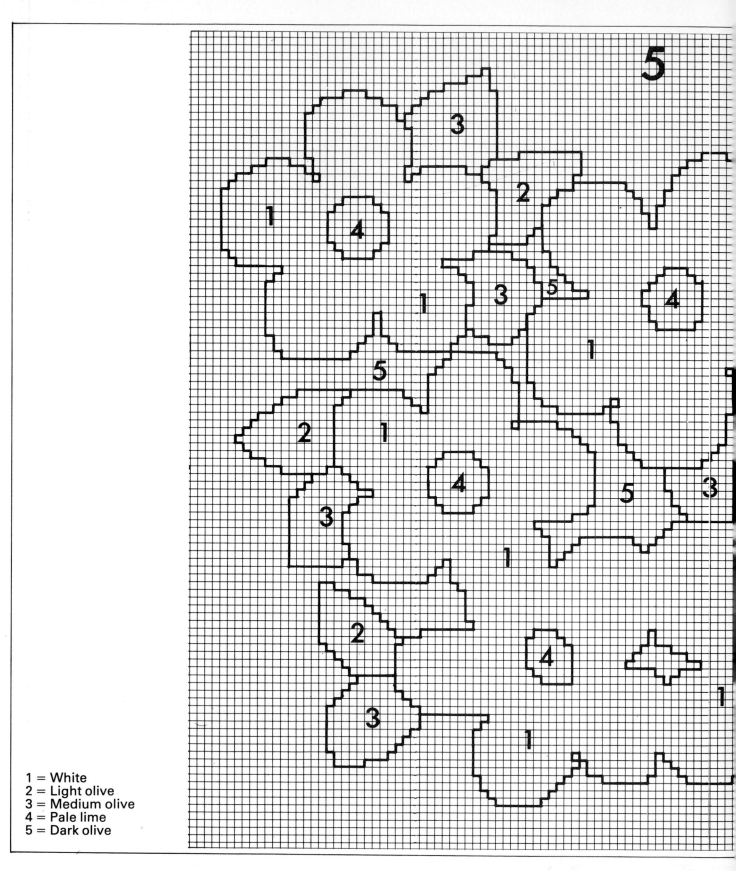

1 = White
2 = Light olive
3 = Medium olive
4 = Pale lime
5 = Dark olive

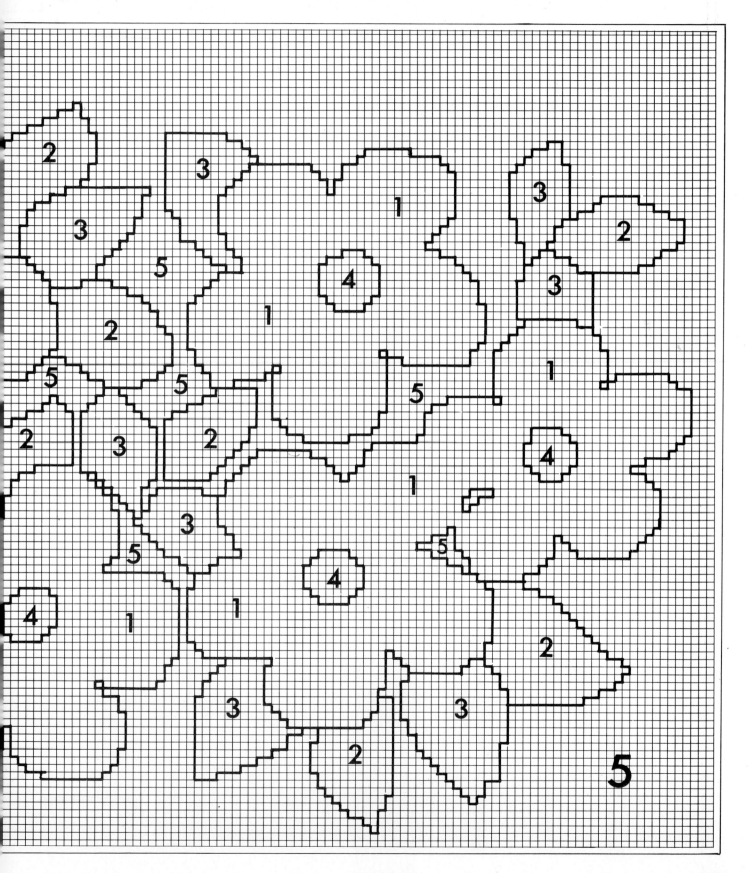

5

19

Primroses

Simplicity of design is the keynote of cross-stitch. This panel is quickly worked in unshaded blocks of color with straight stitches at the flower centers. Use the same design to make a handsome pillow or a wall panel or experiment with different yarns.

Working the design

Mark the widthwise and lengthwise centers of the canvas. In cross-stitch, a rythmical working method gives an even texture. Follow the chart and work in rows one below another. Thread separate needles with each color. Work the stitches and bring the needle up in position ready for that color when it is next needed. Continue working with a second color and needle and complete all stitches across the row working over the previous thread on the back. When the canvas is filled, add the straight stitches at the flower centers as indicated on the chart.

Finishing the pillow

Stretch the finished canvas. Trim the hem to 1½ inches. Turn under a single hem allowance, leaving a canvas edge ½in wide, the width of the braid. Herringbone-stitch the hem to the back of the work and stitch the braid to the edges of the panel.

Turn under edges of the lining fabric to fit the panel, wrong sides together, and baste the pieces together. With right sides together, pin the backing fabric to the pillow front; baste and stitch together on 3 sides. Turn the pillow cover right side out and insert the pillow form. Slip stitch the remaining edge closed.

Size
10½in square

You will need
14in square of Penelope canvas with 10 double threads to 1in
Tapestry yarn in the following colors and quantities: 5 skeins each of dark brown and bright pink, 2 skeins of fuchsia, 1 skein each of orange, yellow/orange, blue, white, light green and dark green
Tapestry needles
1½yd of ½in-wide edging braid in bright pink
12in square of lining fabric
12in square of backing fabric
Matching sewing thread
Sewing needle

Skills you need
Cross-stitch
Straight stitch
Herringbone stitch

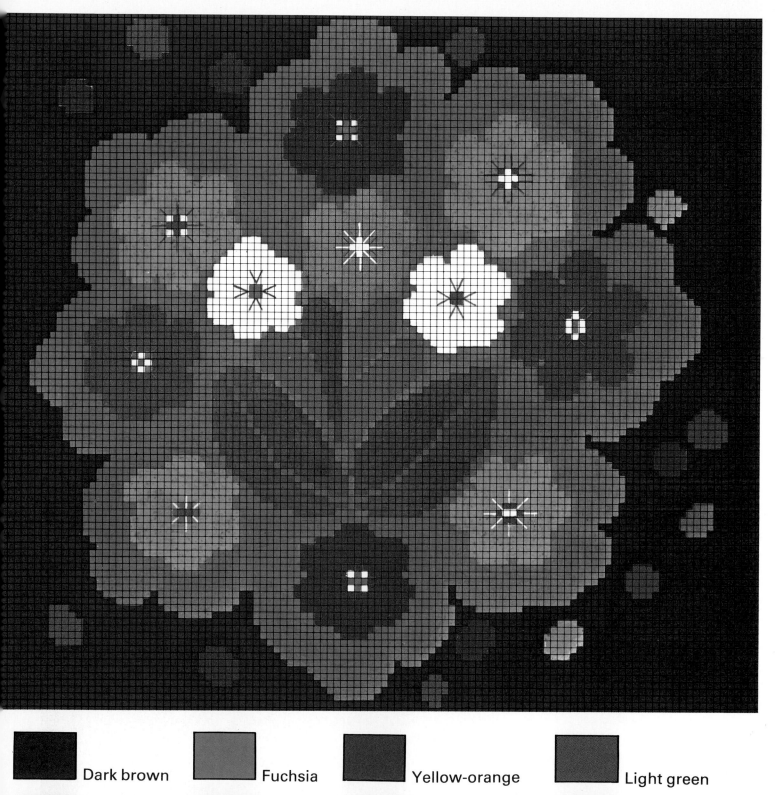

Dark brown	Fuchsia	Yellow-orange	Light green
Bright pink	Orange	Blue	Dark green

Danish rose

Cross-stitch has been used for centuries in traditional folk and peasant embroideries to decorate national costumes and household articles.

Each country has developed its own particular style to such an extent that it is possible to determine where a particular piece of work or design originated. For instance, modern Danish cross-stitch designs usually depict forms in a very realistic manner. The rounded shapes of flowers, birds and animals are embroidered in delicate, pretty colors in carefully selected tones, which when worked together, enhance this realistic effect.

This delightful rose is typical of Danish cross-stitch, and can be used in many exciting ways. Here it has been worked in two ways to create completely contrasting effects. One rose is worked in knitted worsted yarn on coarse canvas to make a pretty pillow; the other, in stranded embroidery floss on fine linen, is mounted as a picture in a tiny gold frame.

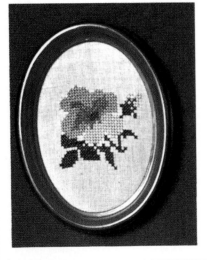

The picture

To work the embroidery
Use the enlarged photograph on page 24 as a chart to work the rose in the center of the linen. Using two strands of embroidery floss, work each stitch over two threads.

To finish the picture
Press the work lightly on the wrong side. Mount on heavy cardboard (see page 146) and frame.

The pillow

To make the pillow
Mark the center of the canvas widthwise and lengthwise. Starting from the center of the design as indicated by the arrow, work the rose over 3 threads, using 2 strands of yarn throughout. When the rose is completed, fill in the background in cream, working across complete rows when possible, until the embroidery measures 14in square.

To finish the pillow, see diagram 4 below.

Size
Rose motif 2⅝ x 2½in

You will need
Piece of linen 8 x 10in, with 24 threads to 1in
1 skein of stranded embroidery floss in each of the following colors: light pink, medium pink, dark pink, yellow, leaf green
Fine tapestry needle

Size
Approx 14in square

You will need
16in square of canvas with 12 threads to 1in
Knitting worsted: 4oz of cream, 1oz each of light pink, medium pink, dark pink, yellow, leaf green
Tapestry needle

Special technique — Making pillow covers

1. Stitch embroidery fabric to backing fabric with right sides together. Leave an opening for turning right side out.

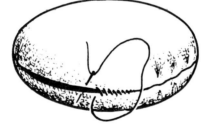

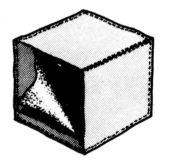

3. Turn right side out and insert pillow pad. Slip stitch the opening.

5. To cover a cube, leave two edges unsewn.

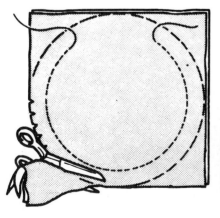

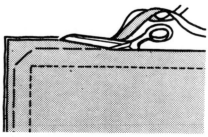

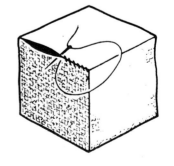

2. For round pillows, trim away the excess fabric and clip into the seam allowance.

4. When trimming square or rectangular pillows, cut across the corner of the seam allowance to reduce the bulk.

6. Slip the pillow cube inside and slip stitch the opening.

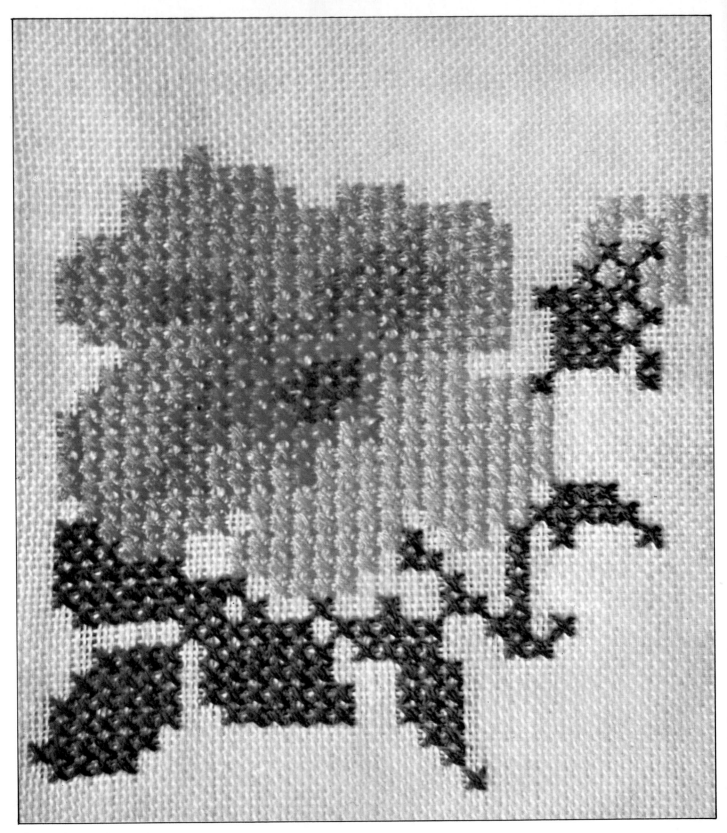

Chart for A Danish Rose

Anemones and pansies

Motifs such as this simple pansy and anemone can be used for a wide variety of items by enlarging or reducing them. Worked on fine canvas or even-weave linen, the designs can be used for everything from miniature pictures for greeting cards to curtain tie-backs. Worked on large-mesh canvas over several threads, they make squares for rugs or pillows.

To work the panels

Mark the center of the piece of canvas each way with lines of basting stitches. Work in cross-stitch over two threads of canvas, following the designs from the center. Use the photographs on pages 26 and 27 as charts.

Turn under the excess canvas and herringbone-stitch the hem in place. If the panels are to be used as pictures, back them with a square of lining fabric; slip stitch it in place.

If both designs are to be incorporated into a single piece of work, allow an extra inch of canvas and extend the background of the anemone to match the pansy.

Make sure that the outer row of border stitches is the same color on each panel and slip stitch the panels together.

Red anemone panel
Size
11 x 12in

You will need
15 x 16in of mono canvas with 10 threads to 1in
Matte embroidery cotton: 1 skein each of orange, rose pink, silver gray and white
2 skeins of pearl cotton no. 3 in poppy red

Purple pansy panel
Size
12 x 13in

You will need
16 x 17in of mono canvas, 10 threads to 1in
Matte embroidery cotton: 1 skein each of dark blue, white and light green
Pearl cotton no 3: 1 skein of red, 2 skeins of purple

Design ideas

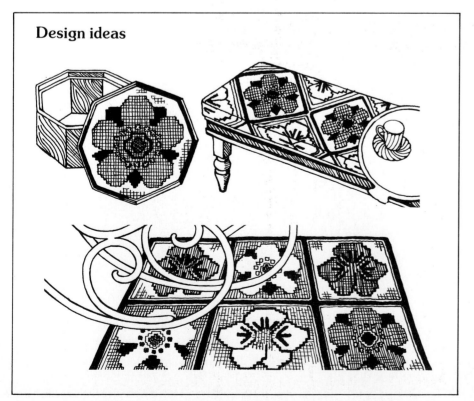

Anemone

26

Pansy

Wild rose pillow

Use this lovely flower on anything from a throw pillow to a baby's blanket.

Size
10in diameter

You will need
⅜yd of 24in-wide dress-weight linen with an even weave, 20 threads to 1in
Stranded embroidery floss in the following colors and quantities:
3 skeins of gold; 1 skein each of white, leaf green and kelly green
Tapestry needle
1yd of cording in a contrasting color
Sewing thread to match fabric
Sewing needle

To work the embroidery
Cut the fabric into two 12in squares. Put one aside to use for the back of the pillow. Bind the edges of the second square with masking tape, or baste the edges under to prevent raveling. Mark the center point with lines of basting in both directions. Work the wild rose from the center, using 3 strands of embroidery floss and working over two threads for each stitch.

To finish
Mark a circle with a 12in diameter on both pieces of linen fabric. Cut out the circles and make the pillow cover as shown on page 23, inserting the cording to finish the edges.

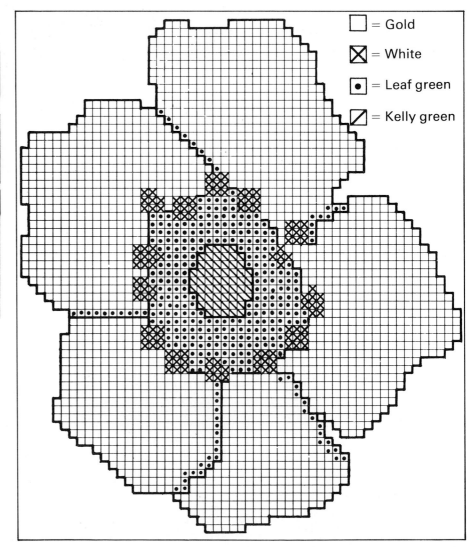

☐ = Gold
☒ = White
⊡ = Leaf green
▨ = Kelly green

28

AROUND
THE
HOUSE

Apple of your eye

This border of apples would look just as pretty on a plain towel. Or work a border on a place mat and make a matching napkin with a single apple in the corner.

You will need
1 evenweave dish towel
1 skein of stranded embroidery floss in each of the following colors: bright red, red-orange, yellow and leaf green
Size 7 crewel needle

Positioning the motifs
Decide where you want to place each apple, and then mark the spot that will be the center stitch of the design (shown in black on the chart).

Working the design
The design is worked with two strands of embroidery floss in the crewel needle. Begin each length of thread with a knot, or with a few tiny stitches on the wrong side.
Start by working the center stitch and build up the apple shape in stitches of different colors, following the chart. Cover an even number of threads with each stitch. The size of each apple will depend on the number of threads covered by each stitch.

Summer scenes

These delightful coasters with their butterfly and flower designs are typical of the freshness and delicacy usually found in Scandinavian table linen designs. If they are worked on a coarser weave fabric than the one used here, the motifs are enlarged and can be used in the corners or in the center to make a tablecloth. A single motif would also make a charming pillow, a patch pocket or, mounted in a small frame, a pretty picture.

Working the mats

For each mat, cut a square of fabric measuring 10 x 10in on the straight grain of the fabric. Prepare the edges for hemstitching by drawing out two threads on all four sides, 2¼in from the edge. (See below). Overcast the edges to prevent raveling.

Refer to the photographs on the following pages as a guide to the placing of each design and work, following the charts. Work cross-stitches over two threads of fabric each way using two strands of floss in the tapestry needle. The solid areas are worked in cross-stitch and the single lines, such as those for the butterflies' antennae and legs, in Holbein stitch.

Finishing the mats

When the embroidery is completed, press on the wrong side over a damp cloth. Cut away the extra fabric to within 1¼in from the drawn threads on each edge. Make a hem all around each mat ¼in deep and miter the corners. Turn up the hem to the very edge of the drawn threads and baste. Secure the hem with hemstitching (see page 40), picking up two drawn threads at a time and pulling the working thread firmly to bunch each group. Be sure to catch the turned-under edge of the hem in each stitch.

Size
6in square

You will need
To make six mats:
⅜yd of 60in-wide evenweave linen with 25 threads to 1in
Stranded embroidery floss in the following colors and quantities: 1 skein each of brown, light orange, medium orange, light mauve, dark pink, light mustard, dark mustard, dark orange, dark mauve, light blue, dark blue, light pink, medium pink
2 skeins each of dark green, light green
Size 24 tapestry needle

Skills you need
Cross-stitch
Holbein stitch
Hemstitching

Special technique —
Withdrawing threads for hemstitching

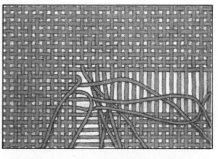

1. Mark the corners of the inner edge of the hem with four pins. Immediately inside this edge, cut and withdraw the thread along each side 2in from each corner.

2. Remove one thread from corner to corner along each side. Continue drawing out threads in this way until you have a border wide enough to suit your embroidery.

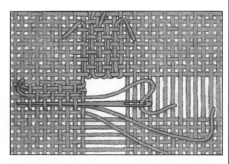

3. Using a fine tapestry needle, darn in all loose threads at the corners for 1½in to secure them. Be careful to take the thread over the top thread as shown. Cut off the loose ends.

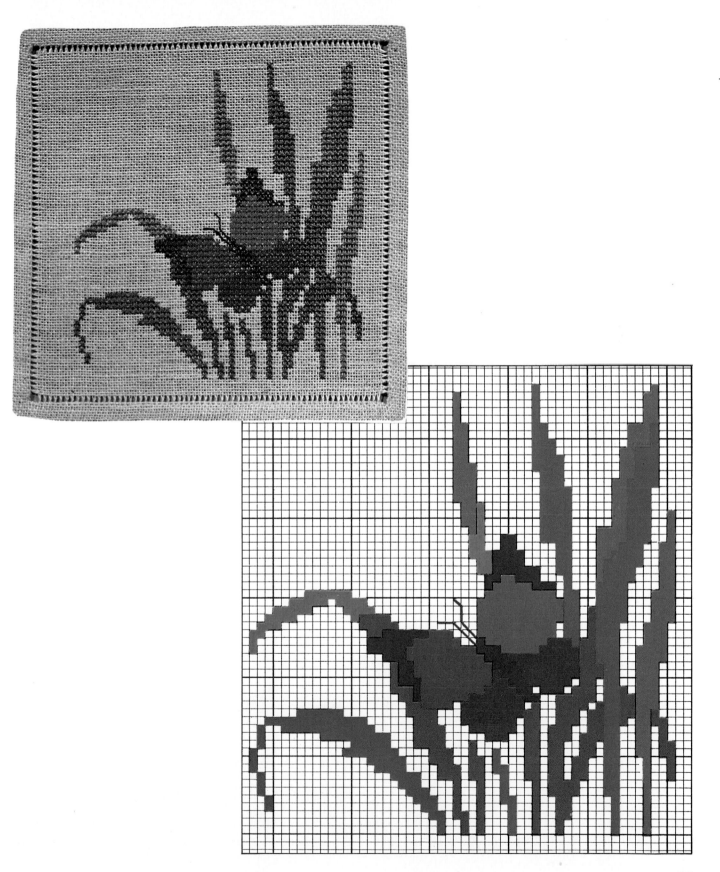

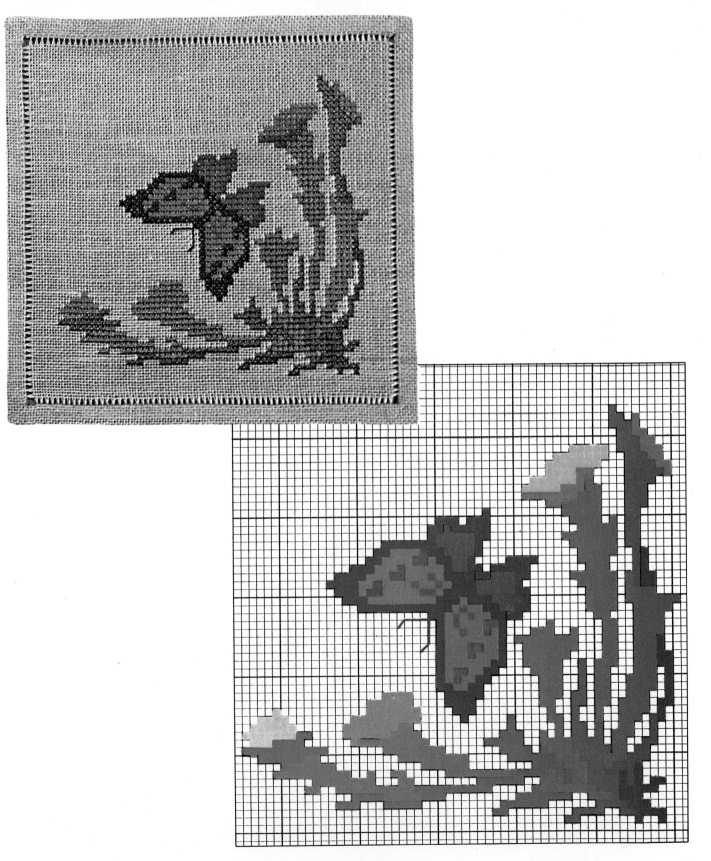

Sophisticated table

These cross-stitched place mats have an ingenious
asymmetrical design which is echoed on the matching napkins.
Used with modern tableware, they provide a smart setting for
any table. Hemstitch the edges first; then work the cross-stitch.

Working the embroidery

Each stitch is worked over 2 fabric threads using 3 strands of embroidery floss throughout.

Napkins

With the napkins laid flat, right side up, count 18 threads to the right of the hemstitching at the lower left-hand corner and 10 threads up from the hemstitching along the bottom. Bring the needle up at this point (see blue arrow) and make the first stitch down diagonally to the right. Complete the cross-stitch with a diagonal stitch in the other direction. Continue working the pattern around all four edges of the napkin, following the chart and working 20 motifs on each side, including both corners.

Place mats

Starting at the hemstitching at the lower left-hand corner, count 17 threads up and 28 threads to the right. Work the first stitch at the point indicated by the arrow. Continue working the pattern for the left side of the place mat, following the chart and working 11 motifs in all.

Starting at the hemstitching at the lower right-hand corner, count 27 threads up and 27 threads to the left. Work the first stitch at this point, indicated by arrow. Continue working the pattern for the right side of the place mat, following the chart and working 11 motifs in all.

Finished size
Place mat 10¾ x 15½in
Napkin 15½in square

You will need
1⅝yd of 36in-wide evenweave cotton with 27 threads to 1in
10 skeins of stranded embroidery floss in a contrasting color
Tapestry needle
Sewing thread to match fabric

Skills you need
Cross-stitch
Hemstitching

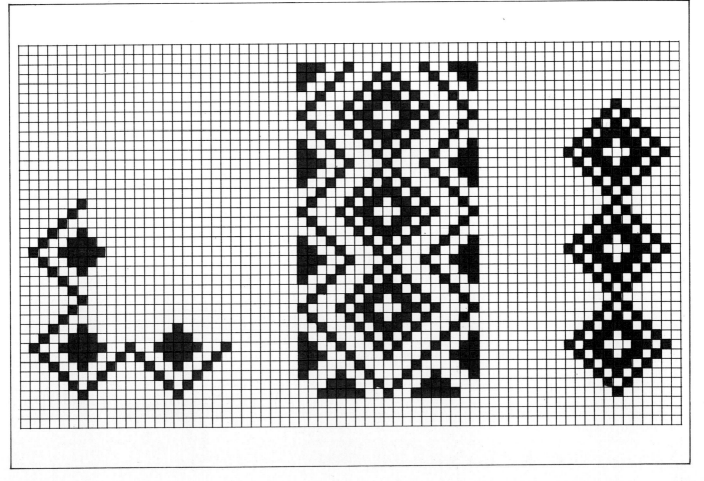

Note

The embroidery can be worked on fabric with fewer or more than 27 threads to 1in, but in this case you must first calculate the space needed for a single repeat of the design and multiply this by the number of motifs desired. It is best then to buy additional fabric and cut the mats and napkins larger than directed below. Overcast the edges to keep them from raveling, work the embroidery and then hem the pieces.

Special technique — Hemstitching the edges

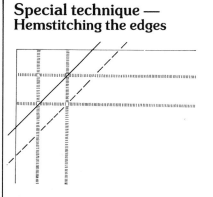

1. *On all four edges of each piece, count in eight threads and carefully withdraw the eighth thread. Count a further 11 threads from the space and withdraw the 11th thread. Cut straight across the corners indicated by the solid line. Fold the diagonal line along the broken line through the point where the inner drawn thread lines intersect. Pin and baste the fold in place.*

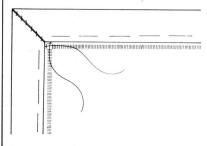

2. *Fold the straight edges of the fabric twice, along each of the withdrawn thread lines. Pin and baste them in place to complete the mitered corners. Withdraw one thread just inside each hemmed edge. Remove the thread only to the inner corner where it meets the other thread. Leave an end about 2in long; thread the end into the hem and cut off the excess thread.*

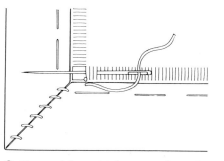

3. *To work hemstitching, work on the wrong side, anchoring the thread under the hem. Begin with a small vertical stitch going through to the right side. Work over the edge and up through the hem edge. Take the needle through the first three threads.*

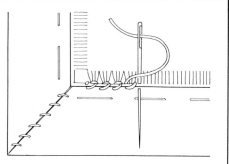

4. *Make a single vertical stitch from the right side to the wrong side, catching in the hem edge. Pull the working thread taut to gather the fabric threads together.*

City life

A boulevard of buildings and trees forms the center of this cheerful tablecloth.

Preparing the fabric
Cut the linen on the grain of the fabric to make a 48in square. Mark the center in both directions with lines of colored basting stitches, following the threads.

Working the embroidery
The chart gives one-eighth of the design, and the center (indicated with a blank arrow) should match the basting stitches. Each background square on the chart represents one stitch worked over three threads.

The design is worked in cross-stitch with the exception of small window areas outlined in backstitch. As always when working cross-stitch, make sure that the crosses lie in the same direction.

Start the design 139 threads down and 1 thread to the right of the black arrow and work the section given. Following the color and position key, repeat the design in reverse from the blank arrow to complete one-quarter of the design, which is one complete size of the tablecloth. Work the three remaining sides in the same way. Press the embroidery lightly on the wrong side.

To finish
Turn under a 1in double hem all around the tablecloth and pin. Miter the corners and baste the hem in position. Using matching sewing thread, slip stitch around all four sides of the hem.

Size
48in square

You will need
1½yd of 50in-wide evenweave linen with 18 threads to 1in
Tapestry yarn in the following colors and quantities: 7 skeins of bright blue; 5 skeins of black; 3 skeins each of leaf green, bright yellow and bright red; 2 skeins each of orange and brown
Tapestry needle
Sewing thread to match fabric

Skills you need
Cross-stitch
Backstitch

Black
Bright blue
Leaf green
Bright yellow } Cross-stitch
Orange
Bright red
Brown
Black backstitch

Wild flowers

This pretty tablecloth is composed of two naturalistic designs of Danish origin set on a diamond trellis and finished with lace to bring charm and style to any dining room.

Size
33in square

You will need
½yd of 60in-wide evenweave linen
with 27 threads to 1in
Danish flower thread in the following
quantities and colors: 1 skein each of
pale pink, soft pink, medium pink, dark
pink, yellow, leaf green, medium
green, pale green, dark green, brown,
light brown
3 skeins each of red and green
Tapestry needle
Embroidery hoop
4yd of decorative straight-edge lace
4yd of lace with a scalloped edge
Sewing thread to match fabric

To work the embroidery

The tablecloth is made of nine 9in squares. Four of these are embroidered with the wild strawberry plant, and five with the square strawberry flower design. The Danish method of working cross-stitch is to work the linen freely in the hand, but you can use an embroidery hoop if you prefer.
Cut a 10in square, following the weave of the linen, and overcast the edges to prevent raveling. Find the center of the linen by basting a vertical and horizontal line of stitches through the square of fabric from the center point on each side. Find the center of the wild strawberry plant motif with the aid of the arrows. Begin the embroidery at the center, working in one strand of Danish flower thread over two threads of linen. Work one area of color at a time, following the charts. Avoid carrying threads across the back of the work; they will be visible from the right side.

To finish

When the embroidery is completed, trim ¼in from each edge of the linen, leaving a 9½in square. Cut the lace into four equal lengths. Finish the edges and insert the lace as shown on page 45. Be sure to arrange the squares in the correct order.
When all nine squares are completed and joined to the insertion lace, finish the edges of the tablecloth with scalloped lace.

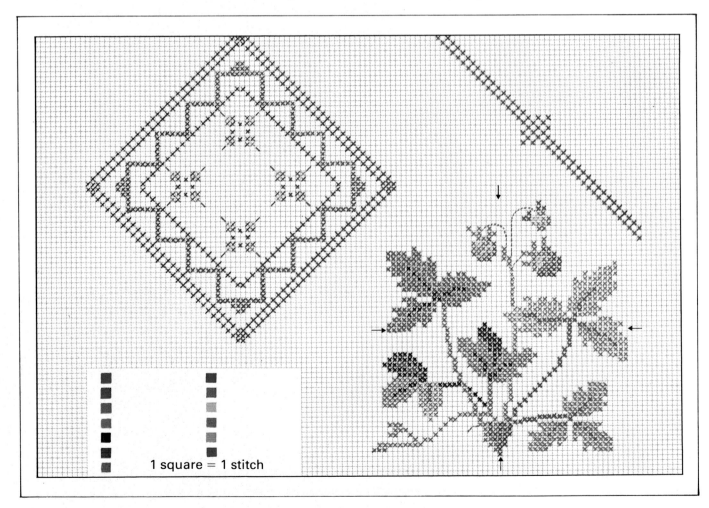

1 square = 1 stitch

Special technique — Lace insertion

1. Once the embroidery is completed, trim the edges of the linen. Taking each edge in turn, fold ¼in of linen to the right side. Finger press along the fold and baste in place, mitering the corners neatly.

2. Take a corner motif and a piece of lace. Pin the lace along the top of the square to cover the raw edge of the linen. Baste in place. Baste another piece of lace to the right-hand edge.

3. Pin and baste the horizontal band of lace to the bottom edge of the second square, and the vertical band to its right-hand edge. Continue adding squares and lace, weaving the lace alternately over and under at intersections, until the squares are all in position. Stitch along both edges of all the pieces of lace and remove basting.

Note

Use a fine linen (27 or 30 threads to 1in) to retain the delicacy of these designs. Coarser linen and other evenweave fabrics can be used to produce a bolder effect if desired.

Work the designs in Danish flower thread, which comes in a range of beautiful colors similar to those produced by natural dyes, or in stranded embroidery floss. Use one strand of Danish flower thread or two strands of stranded embroidery cotton on fine linen, increasing the number of strands to suit coarser fabrics.

Decorative lace adds a pretty finish. Or, use braid to finish the outside edges of a coarser fabric, and a co-ordinated straight-edge lace for the insertions.

Feast of flowers

To adapt this geometric carnation with its stylized borders, use a single carnation along the edge of a place mat with the smaller motif in the corner of a matching napkin.

Size
35in square

You will need
1yd of 36in-wide white evenweave cotton or linen, 20 threads to 1in
Stranded embroidery floss in the following colors and quantities:
2 skeins each of bright green and orange
1 skein of yellow
Tapestry needle
Embroidery hoop
Sewing thread to match fabric

To work the embroidery
Trim the fabric to make a precise square approximately 36in on all sides. Turn the edges under and baste them to prevent raveling. To find the exact center of the fabric, run lines of basting down the center both lengthwise and widthwise.

The center stitch is marked by a black square on the chart. Begin by working it in orange and follow the chart to make one flower motif. Use 3 strands of floss and work over two threads in each direction. Then reverse the design to make another flower opposite the first, starting at the bottom of the flower stem. Now turn the work and make two more flowers at right angles to the first two.

To work the inner border, measure out 9in from the center stitch and begin by working the center stitch of one of the small floral motifs. Work the green border all around; then work the flowers, turning the corners as shown on the chart.

To work the outer border, measure up 3in from the edge of the fabric along one of the basting marker threads and work the center stitch of one of the small flowers. Work as for the inner border.

To finish
Hem the tablecloth on all four sides, mitering the corners.

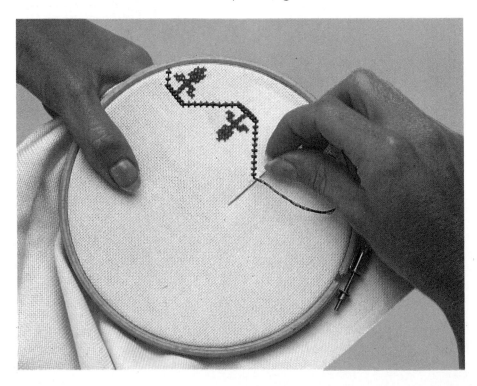

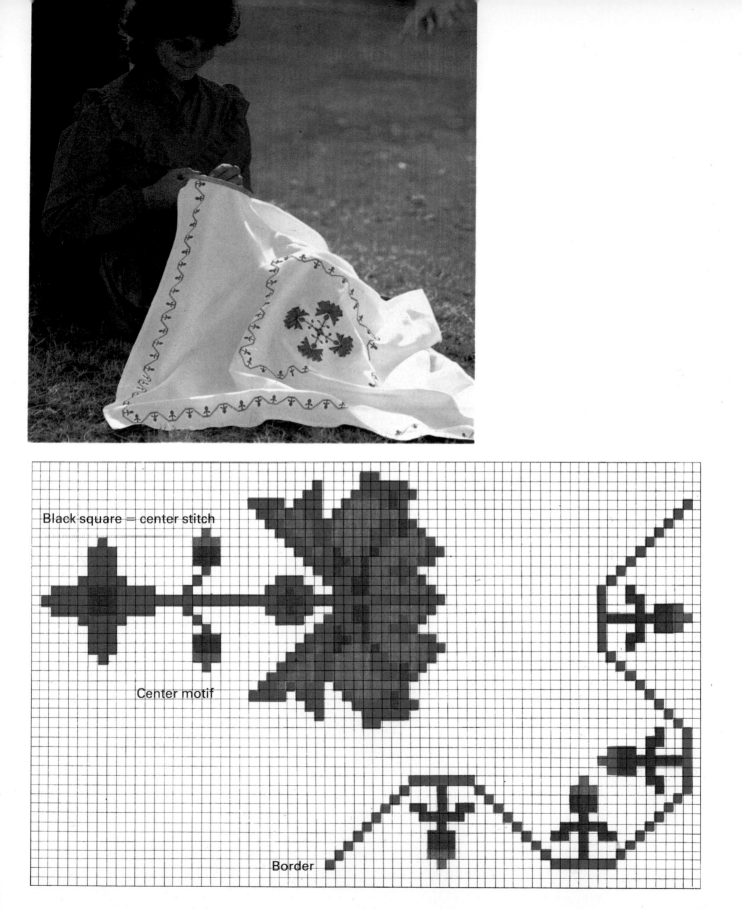

Black square = center stitch

Center motif

Border

Afternoon tea

This beautiful tea cloth will add a touch of elegance to any table. The design is worked alternately in filet crochet and cross-stitch on linen, and the edge is repeated to form a border for the whole cloth.

To make embroidered squares

Cut 13 squares, each measuring 8½ x 8½in, from evenweave fabric. Using 6 strands of floss, work the cross-stitch motif in the center of each square, working in rows from the chart on page 50. Turn under ¼in on all four edges of each square and press down.

Using No. 10 crochet hook and mercerized crochet cotton, work in sc all around each square, working 4sc into each corner and 105sc along each side. These edges will correspond with the edges of the crochet squares.

To make crochet squares

Gauge 27dc (9 blocks or sps) and 9 rows to 2in worked on No. 10 crochet hook. Each square measures 8in after pressing.

To work the crochet

Using No. 10 hook, make 110ch.
1st row 1dc into 8th ch from hook, *2ch, miss 2ch, 1dc into next ch, rep from * to end. 35 sps.
2nd row 5ch to count as first dc and 2ch, 1dc into next st, (2dc into next sp, 1dc into next dc, 2ch, 1dc into next dc) 3 times, *(2ch, 1dc into next dc) 4 times, 2dc into next sp, 1dc into next dc, 2ch, 1dc into next dc, rep from * 3 times more, 2dc into next sp, 1dc into next dc, 2ch, 1dc into next dc, 2dc into next sp, 1dc into next dc, 2ch, 1dc into 5th of 7ch.
Cont in patt, working from chart for rows 3 to 18, then working from row 17 back to row 1.
Finishing round 1ch, 3sc into same st, *3sc into each sp to corner, 4sc into corner sp, rep from * all around, ending with sl st to 1ch. 109sc on each side. Fasten off.
Make 11 more squares.

To make the tablecloth

Overcast the squares together on the wrong side. Place embroidered squares in each corner and alternate them with crochet ones.

Size
43in square

You will need
1yd of 36in-wide evenweave linen, 21 threads to 1in
13 skeins of stranded embroidery floss
9 balls of mercerized crochet cotton to match stranded floss
Tapestry needle
No. 10 crochet hook
Sewing thread to match fabric
Sewing needle

Skills you need
Cross-stitch
Single crochet
Double crochet

To make the edging

Using a No. 10 hook and mercerized crochet cotton, with RS facing, join yarn to any corner.

1st round 8ch, 1dc into same space, *2ch, skip 2sc, 1 dc into next sc, rep from * all around, working (1dc, 5ch, 1dc) into each corner and ending with sl st to 3rd of 8ch.

Cont in patt, working from chart for rounds 2 to 5. Work finishing round of Crochet Square.

Next round *5ch, skip 2sc, 1sc into next sc, rep from * all around, ending with sl st to first of 5ch.

Fasten off.

Press work on the wrong side under a damp cloth, using a warm iron.

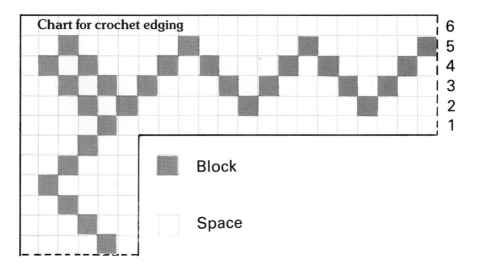

Chart for crochet edging

6
5
4
3
2
1

■ Block

☐ Space

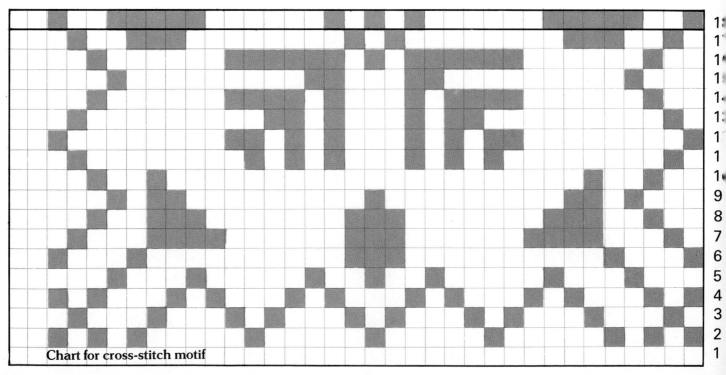

Chart for cross-stitch motif

Star-crossed table

This richly decorated table runner is embroidered in white yarn on a blue background to give a dramatic effect. The design would make a good border decoration for a tablecloth or it could be worked in vertical bands on a curtain.

Size
14 x 50in

You will need
½yd of 60in-wide blue evenweave
linen with 21 threads to 1in
3 skeins of white pearl cotton
Size 16 crewel needle
Sewing needle
Sewing thread to match fabric

Skills you need
Cross-stitch
Holbein stitch

Preparing the fabric
Mark the vertical and horizontal centers of the fabric with basting stitches, following the grain of the fabric.

Working the embroidery
Following the chart, which outlines the top half of each motif, work the design over two threads. The main part of the design is worked in cross-stitch with the fine lines worked in Holbein stitch. The bottom row of stitches shown on the chart should align with the basting thread that runs along the length of the fabric. Reverse the chart to complete each motif. Work 21 complete repeats of the design all along the center of the cloth.

Finishing the table runner
Turn up a 1in double hem around all four edges of the runner and baste in position. Slip stitch in place, mitering the corners neatly.

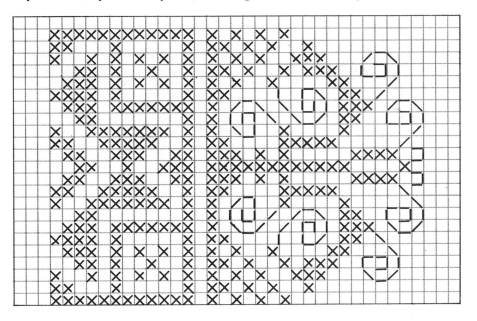

Design ideas

Gingham bright

Brighten a baby's room with this gingham-trimmed sheet and matching pillowcase.

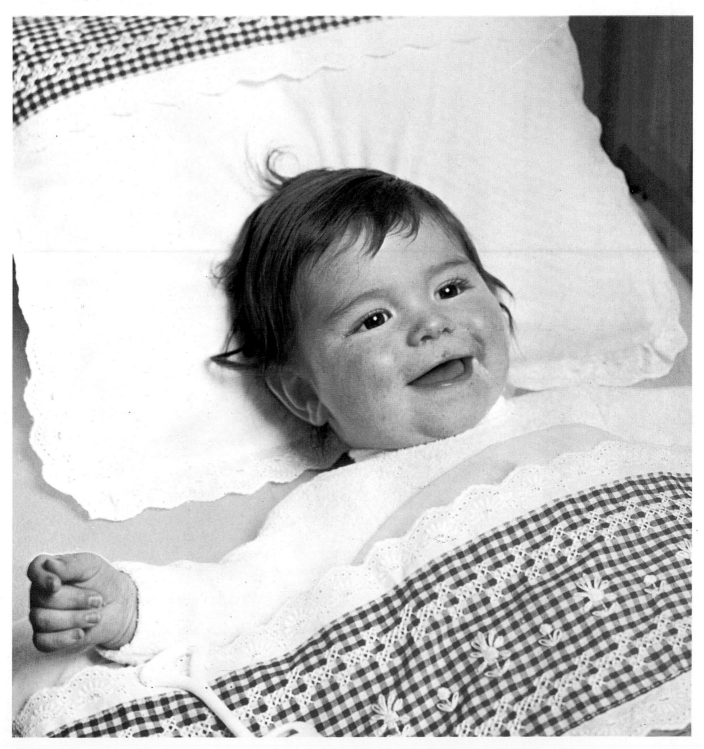

Sizes
Sheet: 40 x 60in
Pillowcase: 14 x 15½in

You will need
White flat sheet and pillowcase to fit a junior bed
⅜yd of 45in-wide red and white gingham with checks ⅛in square
5 skeins of stranded embroidery floss (or 1 skein of pearl cotton) in white
Size 7 crewel needle
5yd of 1½in-wide white eyelet trim
Sewing thread to match fabric
Dressmaker's carbon paper

Skills you need
Cross-stitch
Lazy daisy
Satin stitch
Stem stitch

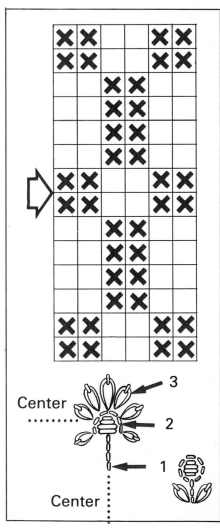

Preparing the fabric
Cut two pieces of gingham, one for the sheet 5½ x 45in and one for the pillow case 5½ x 16½in. Fold both pieces in half both lengthwise and widthwise. Crease both pieces lightly and mark the creased lines with basting.

Working the embroidery
Count seven squares on each side of the horizontal center line and work the cross-stitch borders on the long sides of both pieces of the gingham. Following the chart, start on the basted vertical line at the point indicated by the blank arrow, and work outward in both directions. Each stitch is worked on one square of the check.
Using dressmaker's carbon paper, trace the motifs for the flowers onto the fabric so that dotted lines correspond with the center lines on the gingham. Repeat on the left and right sides along the entire length of the border, spacing them evenly.
Work section 1 of the flowers in stem stitch, section 2 in satin stitch and section 3 in lazy daisy.
Press the embroidery on the wrong side.

Making the sheet
Turn under ½in all around the edges of the gingham and pin. Baste the eyelet trimming in place around the edge of the gingham with the raw edges even on the wrong side. Gather the eyelet to ease it around the corners. Overlap the short ends of the eyelet so that the pattern matches and overcast the raw edges together.
Place the gingham on the right side of the sheet at the top end so that the eyelet forms a ruffle at the top and sides. Baste and stitch in place through all layers.

Making the pillowcase
Carefully rip out the seams of the pillowcase so that you can work with flat pieces.
Turn under ½in along the long edges of the gingham. Baste a piece of eyelet along each of these edges so that the raw edges are even on the wrong side. Stitch the eyelet in place along the top edge.
Stitch a double hem along one long edge of both sections of the pillow-case. This will be the open end of the pillowcase.
Place the gingham on the right side of the front section of the pillowcase so that the side raw edges are even. Baste in place and stitch along the trimmed top edge through all layers.
Place the remaining eyelet along the three untrimmed edges of the right side of the front (gingham-trimmed) pillowcase section so that the raw edges are even and the eyelet is facing in. Gather the eyelet at the corners; ease it to fit and baste in place.
With right sides together, place the back section of the pillowcase on the front section and baste three sides together, enclosing the eyelet on the bottom and the two short sides.
Stitch through all layers, taking ½in seam allowances. Finish the raw edges by zig-zagging or overcasting.
Turn the finished pillowcase right side out and press lightly.

Cross-stitch rugs

Rug canvas produced in different widths and in three sizes with either 3, 5 or 7 holes to 1in, is an excellent base for a stitched rug. Though other woven fabrics such as coarse linen and burlap can be used to make a rug, the stiffened mesh of rug canvas helps to keep the stitches even, and prevents the finished embroidery from stretching out of shape. It is also much easier to count the threads of rug canvas than those of woven fabrics, and the finished effect would be quite different. The threads of rug canvas should be covered completely. Rug yarn can be bought by the hank and is much thicker than knitting yarn. It is hardwearing, mothproofed and colorfast. Use a large blunt-ended rug needle.

Fireside cats

Stitch this striped tabby cat rug in cross-stitch for the family room hearth or to decorate a child's bedroom.

Size
26 x 42in (including the fringe)

You will need
1yd of 30in-wide rug canvas, 3 holes to 1in
1yd of 36in-wide linen or heavy cotton for backing
Rug yarn in the following colors and quantities:
3 hanks of red
2 hanks each dark pink, wild rose, deep blue
1 hank each cornflower, turquoise, blue, yellow, orange, emerald, purple
Rug needle
Button thread
Latch hook (or large crochet hook)

Skills you need
Cross-stitch
Double cross-stitch
Rhodes stitch

To work the embroidery
Mark the center of the canvas in both directions with colored basting thread. Following the chart opposite, count the number of squares required and turn under the canvas to these points. Press the folds well and using buttonhole thread, sew the edges under; then trim them to about three or four threads.

Begin the embroidery in the center, and work the cats in cross-stitch. Each cross-stitch is worked over one intersection of canvas throughout.

Next complete the cat-face border, also in cross-stitch. Work the outer border in Rhodes stitch over 10 threads with lines of cross-stitch in between, again worked over one intersection. Remember to work the individual stitches of Rhodes stitch in sequence, pointing the final stitch in the same direction each time.

Fill in the background with double cross-stitch, working the pink panel first and then the blue border. Fit cross-stitch into the remaining spaces to complete the embroidery.

If necessary, dampen the embroidery and stretch it, leaving it to dry naturally with the right side up.

Add a fringe 4in deep to each short side using red rug yarn if desired.

Cut the backing to size, allowing ¾in extra all around. Turn under and press the allowance, pin the backing in place, wrong sides together, and sew by hand with buttonhole thread to the rug canvas.

Special technique — Hooked fringe

 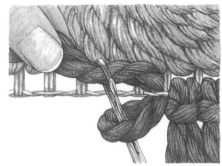 

1. *For a 4in-deep fringe, allow 10in for each length of yarn. Calculate the number required and cut the yarn into equal lengths. With the right side of the rug facing, insert the latch hook as shown, and then fold the yarn in half over the hook.*

2. *Holding the ends of the yarn firmly with the left hand, pull the hook through, closing the latch. Open the latch and twist the hook around the ends. Pull down, as the latch closes, draw the end through the loop on the hook.*

3. *Pull up tightly to make a firm knot (always with the loop on top of the knot). Repeat along the edge of the rug, working into every hole.*

Reverse on center line

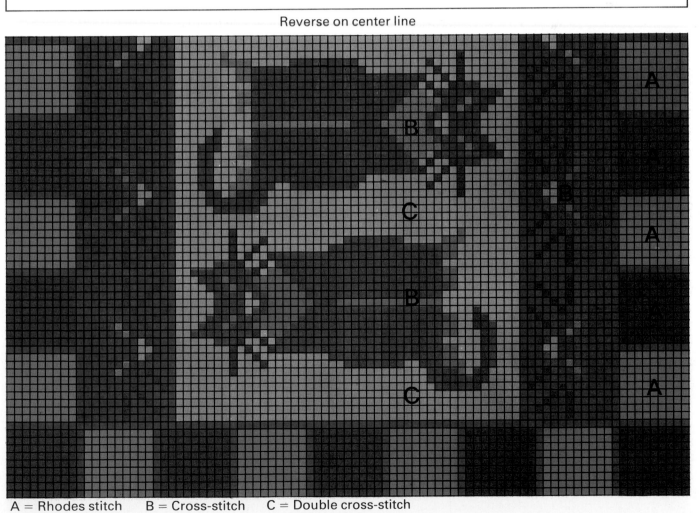

A = Rhodes stitch   B = Cross-stitch   C = Double cross-stitch

Daisy, daisy

This carpet of Marguerita daisies is worked in one piece to make stretching and finishing it simpler.

Size
Approx. 36 x 48in

You will need
1⅜yds of 39in-wide rug canvas, 4 holes to 1in
Rug yarn in the following colors and quantities: 70oz pine green, 32oz white, 26oz kelly green, 6oz yellow, 4oz mustard
5 rug needles
Button thread
4¾yd of 1in-wide rug binding

Skills you need
Cross-stitch
Herringbone stitch

To work the rug
Mark the lengthwise and crosswise centers of the canvas. Count the number of stitches out from the center and work from the chart. Each square represents one stitch. Work straight across in rows, so that you stitch the background and the pattern together. Keep the needles threaded with the five colors. On reaching the end of one color, count the stitches and bring the threaded needle to the front where it is next needed. Then work in the new color, which will automatically cover the strand at the back.

To finish
Stretch the rug into shape. Turn under 3 or 4 rows of spare canvas along each edge and, using button thread, herringbone-stitch the hem in place on the underside of the rug. Trim away excess canvas, especially at the corners, or the rug will not lie flat. Finish with rug binding.

Rainbow shades

This colorful rug will be an attractive long-lasting feature in any room in your home.

Size
28 x 48in

You will need
1½yd of 28in-wide rug canvas with 5 holes to 1in
Rug yarn in the following colors and quantities: 15oz leaf green; 8oz rust; 6oz each of kelly green, peacock blue, raspberry pink, ice blue and pale pink; 4oz buttercup yellow
Tapestry needle

Skills you need
Cross-stitch
Braid stitch
Overcasting stitch

To work the embroidery

Turn under eight threads of canvas along one short edge, folding the canvas along the ninth thread from the raw edge.

Begin working the rug at the folded short edge, working the first four rows through both layers of the canvas and leaving the thread on the edge unworked (see diagram 1). The rug is worked in cross-stitch, with each cross worked over four thread intersections. Make sure that the upper half of each cross slants in the same direction.

Work four rows of leaf green along the whole width of the canvas, then work a few more rows of four stitches along both the long edges to position the design on the canvas (see diagram 2).

Continue working the design of one quarter of the rug, following the chart overleaf for color placement. When one-quarter of the design is completed, you should have 45 stitches across the width of the canvas (including the center stitch marked by the double broken line) and 75 along its length.

Complete one half of the rug by reversing the chart along the horizontal edge marked by the double broken line (see diagram 3).

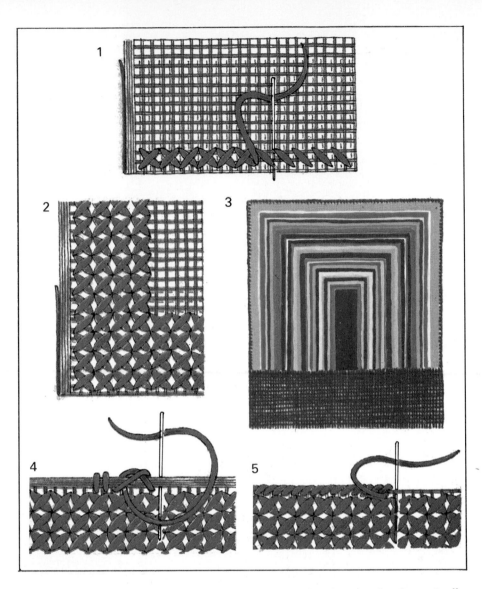

Now work the other half of the rug, reversing the diagram both vertically and horizontally. Leave the last four rows of the design unworked.
Count off nine canvas threads, then fold under the canvas along the ninth thread. Align the mesh carefully and press the fold firmly in place.
Work the last four rows through both layers of canvas. Trim off any surplus canvas that extends beyond the stitching on the underside of the rug.

To finish
Work braid stitch in leaf green along both edges of the rug, working with the wrong side facing (see diagram 4). Work a few upright stitches to anchor the thread, then insert the needle in the next hole from back to front; go over the edge and into the fourth hole to the right, back into the second hole, forward to the fifth hole and so on. Finish with two or three upright stitches. Darn the ends of the yarn into the work.
Work overcasting stitch in leaf green along both short edges of the rug to cover the folded canvas edges (see diagram 5).
Steam press the rug and pull it into shape.

A = Leaf green   B = Pale pink   C = Raspberry pink   D = Ice blue

62

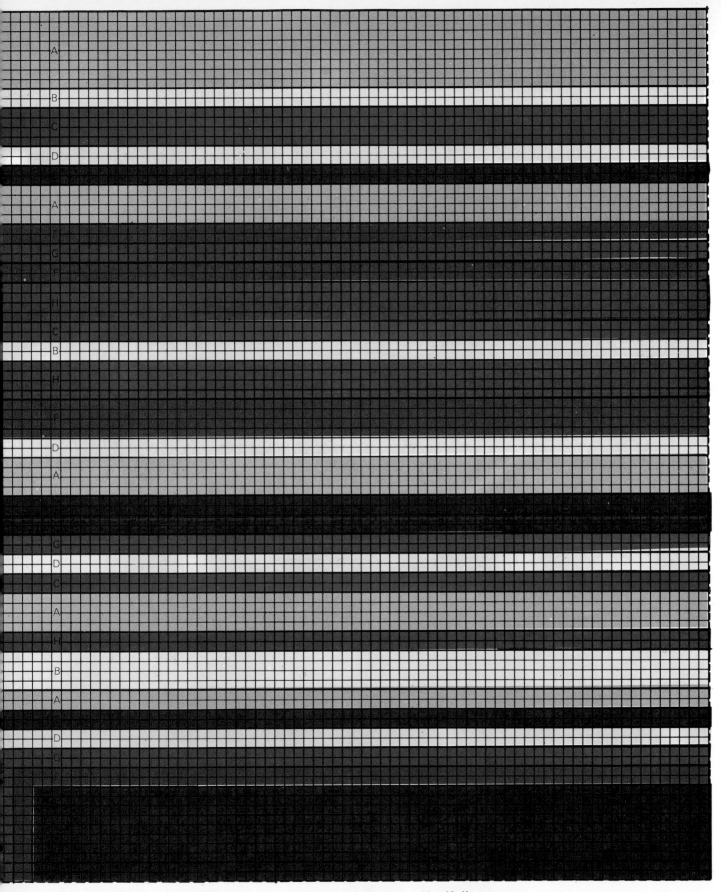

E = Peacock blue   F = Rust   G = Buttercup yellow   H = Kelly green

CROSS-STITCH
IN
FASHION

Embroidery is an excellent way to add your own distinctive touch to a garment. Monograms are perhaps the most common form of embroidery on clothing, but the range of suitable styles and designs is virtually limitless. Before you embroider a piece of clothing you should give careful thought to the positioning of the work. It should look like an integral part of the garment's design, not something stuck on in an arbitrary way. Use the embroidery to highlight some feature of the garment, such as a yoke, a cuff or a patch pocket. If, however, the garment already has plenty of detail in its construction, adding embroidery may produce a fussy look. For the same reason, embroidery is usually confined to solid-color fabrics. Exceptions are fine checked gingham, which lends itself to cross-stitch, and some fine stripes. Also, you can use embroidery to make the design "stand out" on chosen parts of the fabric pattern.

Any evenweave fabric can be used for cross-stitch: cotton, lawn, organdy, linen, or evenweave synthetics.

Provided you use an evenweave fabric, working a pattern is a simple matter of counting threads and following a chart or pattern. Choose threads according to the fabric—for example, stranded embroidery floss or pearl cotton on linen, crewel yarn on lightweight wool, silky or metallic textured threads for evening wear.

Cross-stitch designs

Cross-stitch is well-suited to clothing—particularly to informal clothes. For centuries it has been used on peasant costume in central Europe and Asia, often in highly intricate patterns. Its angular shape gives it a crisp look, enhanced by the use of bright, clear colors on white fabric, but it can easily be used for graceful curved shapes and lines. By using shades of the same color in a design, you can even suggest depth.

Suitable designs are easy to find. Peasant motifs abound, especially trees or flowers, birds, insects and animals. Your library probably has books containing designs already charted for cross-stitch or needlepoint. Or you could use a stencil design or perhaps a photograph or drawing of a plant, animal or object, provided it has a clear shape that will make it easily recognizable when it has been stitched.

General rules of dress embroidery

In some cases the embroidery is worked after the garment is completed—for example, if it covers a seam. More often it is worked on the pattern pieces before assembling, so that you are working on a flat surface and there is a minimum amount of fabric to handle. Work across seam allowances so that the embroidery goes right into the finished seamline.

If the stitches can be worked in the hand, you can cut out the pieces as usual and then work the embroidery. If, however, you need to use a frame, you must use a different method. After pinning on the pattern, draw or baste around the pieces to be embroidered, right on the cutting line. Remove the pattern. Lay the frame over the area to be embroidered and see if there is enough excess fabric outside the cutting line to fill the frame. If so, cut around the piece, allowing the necessary margin. If the cutting layout does not permit this, remove the adjacent pattern piece(s) and work the embroidery on the uncut fabric. Then cut out the pattern and proceed. You can also add embroidery to ready-made clothes, provided you plan the design and placement very carefully.

Nordic beauty

Cross-stitch features in traditional peasant embroidery of many countries, with motifs inspired by insects, flowers, animals and trees. Use them to give an individual look to clothes.

This dress yoke has been worked in a Scandinavian design. The cross-stitch sections are divided by rows of satin stitch blocks, and the stylized floral motifs are linked with backstitch.

The dress is made in evenweave linen and the embroidery has been worked in stranded embroidery floss in pink and brown.

The design would be very attractive worked in a dark thread on a fabric of the same color in a pale shade, such as brown on beige or navy blue on powder blue.

Any individual row of the chart could be used to decorate the cuffs, to make a border around the hem or to make a belt.

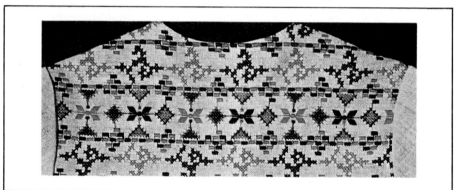

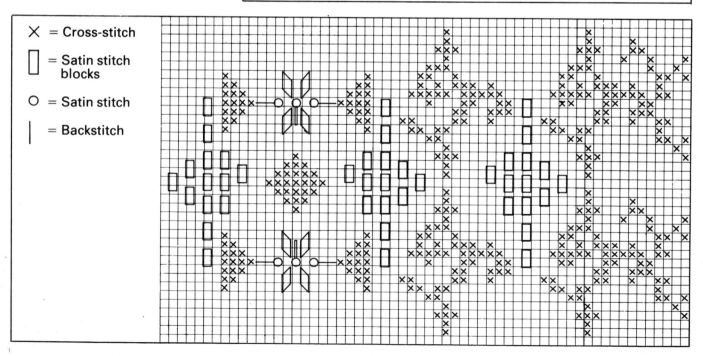

X = Cross-stitch

▯ = Satin stitch blocks

O = Satin stitch

| = Backstitch

Moths and flowers

This moth design looks very pretty on the plain front yoke of a dress or tunic. Work it on a simple cocktail dress in silver or gold metallic thread for a shimmering effect.

Because of its depth, this unusual design is ideal for a border for the hem of a skirt or a dress. We have worked our border in pink, gold and green on a plain, evenweave linen with 18 threads to one inch. Each stitch is worked over two threads.

Worked on a finer fabric, the design could be adapted to make a spectacular belt. It could be worked as a wide border on a sheet, with the moth worked on matching pillowcases. Embroidered on a linen that harmonizes with solid-color curtains, it would make beautiful tie-backs for a bedroom.

The design is shown actual size so that the photograph can be used as a working chart.

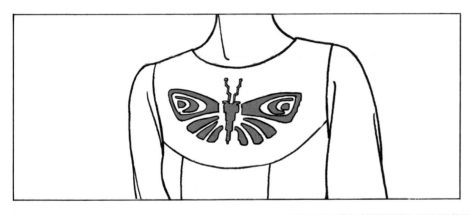

67

Floral geometry

This simple motif is very adaptable. The secret lies in deciding how much of the design can be used effectively.

To work the embroidery

To work the motif as shown on the blouse, five colors of stranded embroidery floss are needed. We have used light jade green, dark jade green, medium rose pink, dark rose pink, and black.

The detail from the design which has been used on the sleeves has been worked in dark pink, medium pink and black.

Ways to adapt cross-stitch

There are numerous ways that the design can be adapted for other uses. Work the entire motif in the center of a bright-colored tablecloth and repeat the border area around the edges. Napkins could be made in a contrasting color, such as gold napkins with a gray-green cloth, and with the embroidery worked in the same shades as the tablecloth. Keep the embroidery on the napkins relatively simple; the stylized floral motif alone echoes the feeling of the larger piece. The motif could be repeated all over a bedspread or worked across the top on a border edging, working the motif in thick embroidery thread on coarse linen.

For a smaller piece of embroidery, work the border pattern alone on a strip of vibrant-colored silk as a hatband . . . perfect trim for a large, floppy hat in felt or straw. Or, work the border pattern along one side edge of a set of place mats and the simplified flower on matching napkins.

Work the whole motif as a repeat around the edge of a full skirt or as a panel down the front of a dress. The single central flower motif could be embroidered on a knitted or crocheted sweater—or try the motif as a pattern for needlepoint, enlarged for a brilliant pillow or on fine canvas for a beautiful accessory such as a compact case.

The birds and bees

This simple blouse made from cheesecloth is made special with embroidered bird and animal motifs and then gathered into an easy-fitting style. The sleeves, neck and waist are fastened with soft cotton cords made in the same colors as the embroidery.

Size
To fit 34 to 36in bust

You will need
1⅝yd of 36in-wide cheesecloth or other lightweight cotton
Stranded embroidery floss in the following quantities and colors:
2 skeins each of light pink, dark pink, red, light blue, leaf green and dark green
1 skein of medium pink
Crewel needle
Embroidery hoop
Sewing thread to match fabric

Skills you need
Cross-stitch
Honeycomb smocking
Buttonhole stitch

To work the embroidery
Cut 2 pieces, each measuring 24 x 36in, for the front and back. Cut straight across the cheesecloth with the selvages at top and bottom. Cut two more pieces for the sleeves, each measuring 20 x 36in.

To prevent raveling, the embroidery is first worked on these rectangular sections which are then cut to shape before assembling the blouse. Mark the center of each piece with a vertical line of basting which should correspond with the center lines marked on the position chart.

Following the stitch diagram, the color key and the position chart for each design, work the embroidery on the blouse in cross-stitch using three strands of floss throughout. The neck edge is finished with five rows of honeycomb smocking using four strands of floss.

Beginning with the front of the blouse, place the embroidery hoop in position on the fabric and work Motif 1.

Choose an embroidery hoop large enough to fit comfortably around the motif to be worked. Try to prevent the embroidery from becoming trapped between the two rings, as the strain will pull the designs out of shape.

Remember that cheesecloth is semi-transparent, so when starting and finishing, the thread should be kept as neat as possible. Trim all loose ends and do not carry threads across the back, or they will show through on the right side.

When the embroidery is completed, press each section gently on the wrong side.

To assemble the blouse
Following the chart carefully, cut each piece to shape. Curve the front and back neck edge as shown, and make a slight curve around the top of the sleeves. Both sleeves are the same shape.

With right sides together, pin the sleeve to the front and back sections and stitch the raglan seam. Trim the seam to ¼in and finish the raw edge. Repeat for the other sleeve.

Trim the lower edge of both sleeves. Match the sleeve seam to the side seam and trim the lower edges of the front and back sections.
With right sides together, begin at the wrist edge and stitch the sleeve and side seam in one continuous procedure. Finish the seam as for the raglan seam above. Repeat for the other side.
Make a ⅜in double hem on the sleeve edges and on the bottom edge of the blouse. Topstitch and press.

To work the smocking
Loosely overcast the raw edge all around the neck. With the wrong side facing, turn under a single 2½in hem and baste close to the edge. Turn the blouse right side out and, beginning at the center front, make six rows of basting, with stitches ⅜in long, spaced evenly across each row.
Follow the diagram and baste each line an equal distance apart. Begin with a knot, baste along the row and unthread the needle, leaving the end loose. Pull up the gathering threads as tightly as the fabric will allow and knot them together in pairs. Arrange the folds evenly.
For the smocking, follow the stitch diagram and begin at the center front, using four strands of floss throughout. The size of the honeycomb stitch is determined by the ⅜in space made between the rows of basting.
Complete five rows of honeycomb stitch in the colors shown on the chart. Remove the basting.

To make the neck opening
To make the opening at the center front neck, cut the cheesecloth to within ¾in of the top motif. Make a small rolled hem between the finger and thumb, and hand-sew it with matching thread.

To finish
Using stranded embroidery floss, cut one 3yd length each of light pink, dark pink and dark green. To make cords for the sleeves, see page 79.
Make two small eyelet holes on the top of the wrist just above the sleeve hem about ½in apart. Finish the edges with buttonhole or blanket stitch. Cut a small slit in the sleeve hem and finish the edges.
Thread the cord through the sleeve hem to tie on the outside of the sleeve as shown. Knot the ends to form a tassel. Repeat for the other sleeve.
To make a cord tie for the neck, cut one 4yd length each of red, light blue and leaf green. Make as for sleeves and thread through the neck edge.

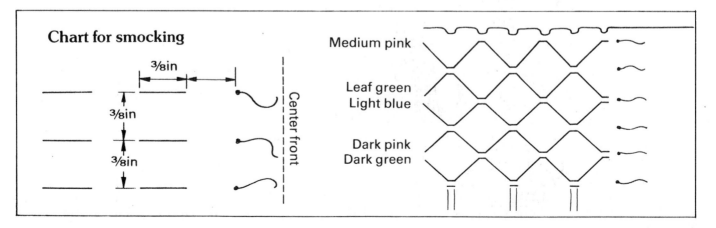

Chart for smocking

⅜in

⅜in

⅜in

Center front

Medium pink

Leaf green
Light blue

Dark pink
Dark green

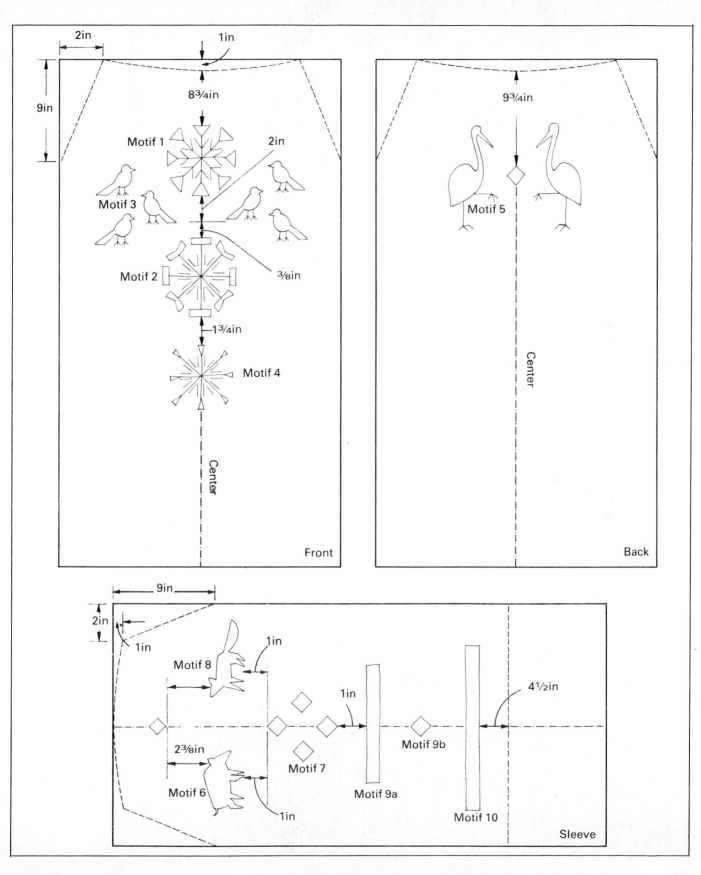

2in

1in

8¾in

9in

Motif 1

2in

Motif 3

Motif 2

⅜in

1¾in

Motif 4

Center

Front

9¾in

Motif 5

Center

Back

9in

2in

1in

Motif 8

1in

1in

Motif 7

Motif 9b

4½in

2⅜in

Motif 6

Motif 9a

1in

Motif 10

Sleeve

73

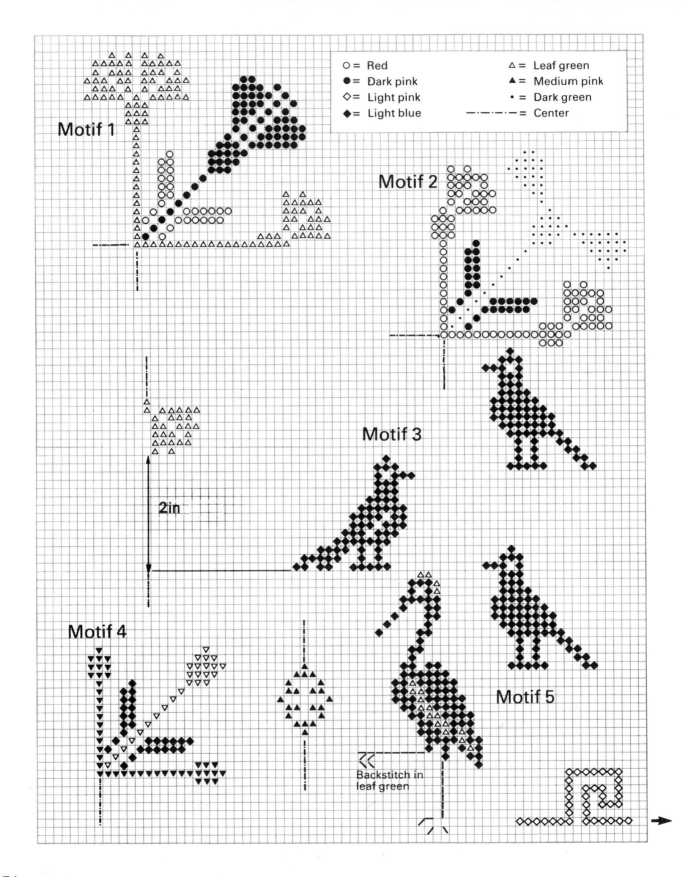

Motif 1

Motif 2

Motif 3

Motif 4

Motif 5

O = Red
● = Dark pink
◇ = Light pink
◆ = Light blue
△ = Leaf green
▲ = Medium pink
• = Dark green
—·—·— = Center

2in

Backstitch in
leaf green

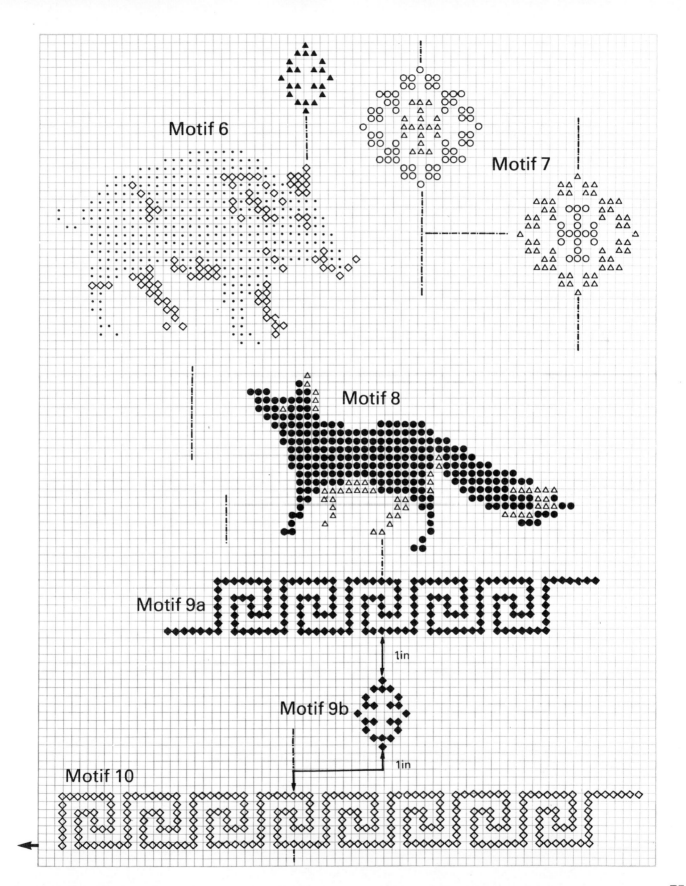

Motif 6

Motif 7

Motif 8

Motif 9a

1in

Motif 9b

1in

Motif 10

Traditional charm

Use a ready-made blouse, or adapt the pattern on page 71 to make this charming summer top.

You will need
Blouse made of evenweave cotton
Stranded embroidery floss: 4 skeins each of dark blue and light blue
Tapestry needle
Embroidery hoop

**Special technique —
Sewing through canvas**

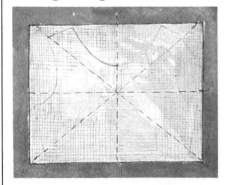

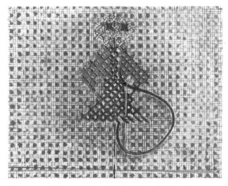

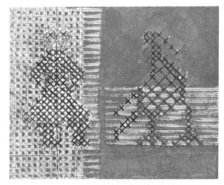

1. *Cut a piece of canvas slightly larger than the area of the cross-stitch design or the area of the fabric to be covered. Baste in place on the embroidery fabric, aligning the threads of the canvas with the grain of the fabric.*

2. *Work the cross-stitch through the canvas and the background fabric, bringing the needle up in a hole and working each stitch over a pair of threads. Stitch evenly and do not split the canvas threads.*

3. *When the cross-stitch is completed, remove the basting, unravel the canvas threads and ease them out from the embroidery one by one. Cut the canvas between each motif to make this process easier.*

To work the embroidery

If you are using a ready-made blouse, you might find it easier to open the underarm seam carefully about halfway up the sleeve so that you can work with the piece flat.

Run a line of basting up the center of the flattened sleeve. Begin the cross-stitch at the center line, working with six strands of floss throughout. Follow the chart and work out to the edge in both directions. When the embroidery is completed, stitch the underarm seam along the original seamline. Repeat for the other sleeve.

Mark the center front of the blouse with a line of basting and work the neckline design, following the chart. Press the completed embroidery on the wrong side.

If you are making the blouse, finish it as shown on page 70.

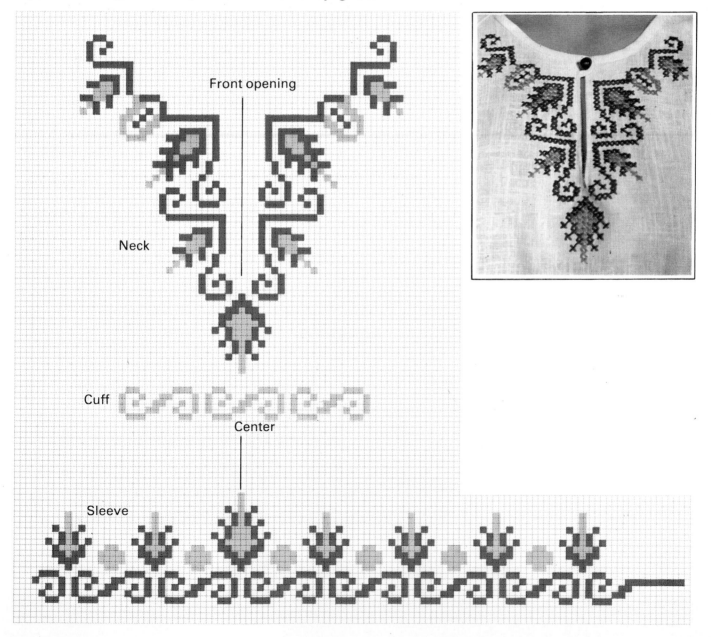

Front opening

Neck

Cuff

Center

Sleeve

Balkan beauty

This attractive peasant blouse is embroidered with traditional flower border designs typical of those worn in parts of Romania. Alternate the two borders below, or adapt any of the designs shown overleaf.

You will need
Plain peasant-style blouse made of evenweave cotton, about 50 threads to 1in
Stranded embroidery floss in the following colors and quantities:
3 skeins of red, 1 skein each of black and blue
Crewel needle

Skills you need
Cross-stitch
Holbein stitch

Special technique — Making a twisted cord

1. *Use different types of yarn to achieve different effects and vary the number of strands to achieve different weights of cord. Take the required number of strands, cut to three times the length of the finished cord and knot each end.*

2. *Fasten one end of the cord around a door handle, put it in a drawer or slip it over a pencil and anchor it in a convenient place. Holding the strands taut, rotate until the strands are tightly twisted.*

3. *Fold in half at the center and knot the ends together. Holding the knot, give the cord a sharp shake and even out the twists by smoothing the cord from the knotted end. Re-knot at the fold and cut to make a neat tassel.*

Note

The cuffs and neck border can be worked on separate pieces of fabric or ribbon and attached if you wish.

To work the embroidery

Mark the position of the borders with basting stitches before beginning the embroidery. Two different borders are used, border A on the neck and cuff bands and on the sleeves, and the border B on the front opening and as the center border on the sleeves.

Position the embroidery on the front of the blouse ⅝in from the front opening. Work down 6in from neck edge.

To position the three borders on the sleeves, center one border on the shoulder and work the others 1¼in away on each side. Work down 7in from the neck edge.

Work the embroidery using two strands of floss over four threads of fabric. Do not carry the thread across the back of the work from one area of color to the next, or they will show through the delicate white fabric.

To finish

Place the finished embroidery on a soft cloth or towel and press on the wrong side with a damp cloth to make the stitches stand out from the background fabric.

If you are embroidering a ready-made blouse and working the cuffs and neck border separately, work them in the same way to the length of the parts of the garment which you are decorating. Turn under a ¼in hem on both long edges of all pieces and press down. Baste each border in place and slip stitch to finish.

Substitute any of these attractive border patterns, or arrange them in a different way to make a colorful blouse of your own design.

Note

Traditional Balkan blouses often have bands of embroidery around the shoulder of a raglan sleeve. Borders can be worked down a sleeve from the neck as shown, or around the sleeve in a wide band. These bands of embroidery are often very elaborate and more solid.

Another feature of traditional peasant blouses is the panels of embroidery on the front of the blouse. Extend the borders on each side of the front opening so that they form a complete panel from the neck to the hem. Again, a geometric border could be used.

Use some of the small designs, or choose small parts of a larger design as spot motifs to embroider at random on the front, back or sleeves of the blouse if you wish.

These designs also make attractive decorations for table linens, handkerchiefs and curtain tie-backs.

South of the border

This kind of colorful embroidery was traditional in Mexico before the Spanish invasion left its marks on Indian crafts. Each village jealously guarded its own designs and colors, so it is fairly easy to trace a piece of antique embroidery back to its original source. The *huipil,* or overblouse, was often embroidered with big bold designs worked in cross-stitch and with imitation seams called *randas.*

Size
To fit 34 to 38in bust

You will need
1¼yd of 54in-wide white evenweave wool, with 20 threads to 1in
Pearl cotton no. 3 in the following quantities and colors:
3 skeins each of pink and yellow
2 skeins each of red and blue
1 skein each of green, orange and violet
Tapestry needle
10in-diameter embroidery hoop
8in of ½in-wide white seam binding
Sewing thread to match fabric
Dressmaker's graph paper

Skills you need
Cross-stitch
Satin stitch

More design ideas

Use one or more of the border patterns to make a bright-colored belt to cheer up a plain skirt or dress. Add a deep border with rows of motifs worked around the hem of a full skirt for an ethnic look. Stitch a delicate border around a scarf of handkerchief. Embroider a small neck purse in an openweave fabric like Binca cloth; use cross-stitch on the front and add beads to the handle. Make bead and thread tassels for a finishing touch. It can be worn around the neck or across the shoulder to hold loose change or precious trinkets.

Note

An evenweave fabric provides the best background for cross-stitch, but bear in mind that the finer the fabric, the finer the finished embroidery will be. If you use a fabric different from the one specified in the pattern, choose one with more threads to 1in. This makes the embroidery slightly smaller, but does not affect the rest of the garment. A fabric with fewer threads to 1in would give a larger motif, but the design would then be too big to fit around the neck and sleeve hems. Wool, linen or cotton can be used, but choose a soft fabric so that the garment hangs well. Single strands of pearl cotton give a colorful, shiny effect and are ideal for working cross-stitch; stranded embroidery floss would be a good substitute if you want a slightly more matte finish. Fine tapestry yarn could also be used.

To work the embroidery

Scale up the pattern pieces in the graph opposite, in which one square equals 1in. Transfer the pattern to dressmaker's graph paper and cut it out. Pin in position on the fabric, placing the pattern pieces on a fold as indicated. With a contrasting color, mark the outline of the blouse all around with basting.

Mark the center back and front, the shoulder lines and the positions of the embroidery with lines of basting.

Remove the pattern pieces from the fabric. Cut out the neck facing only. Work all the embroidery **before** cutting out the blouse. Following the chart and color key, begin at the center front with the pink and yellow border, working each cross-stitch over three threads of fabric. Use the embroidery hoop and move it around as necessary. Complete the front panel.

Begin each randa at the shoulder neck edge, starting with blue pearl cotton and working as shown in the Special technique. Work the pink and yellow cross-stitch border around the back neck edge and along each cuff edge. When the embroidery is completed, lightly press on the wrong side.

To make the blouse

Cut out the blouse with pinking shears. Zig-zag along all the raw edges. Pin, baste and stitch the neck facing to the blouse with right sides together, taking a ⅝in seam allowance. Trim the seam allowance in half and clip corners. Turn facing to wrong side. Hemstitch facing in place. With right sides together and taking ⅝in seam allowances, stitch side seams, reinforcing the dolman sleeve curves with seam binding. Pin and baste a 4in-long piece of seam binding over the center of the stitching line around the underarm curve on one side of the sleeve. Stitch the underarm seam down the center of the binding. Clip the seam allowance at the curve, and be very careful not to cut into the binding. Press the seam open. If necessary, finish the cut edge of the clipped notches to prevent raveling. Make a 1¼in turning on each cuff and a 1in turning on the bottom edge; hem in place. If you prefer to use animal designs to geometric ones, choose one of the stylized designs on pages 74 or 75. Pick one of the individual designs and repeat it as a border around the neckline and cuffs, or replace one of the original square motifs in the center panel with one of the straight-stitched randa motifs. For a more delicate effect, you may prefer to work with a finer evenweave fabric, using two strands of stranded floss. But for an authentically Mexican look, team up a bright background fabric with thread in primary colors.

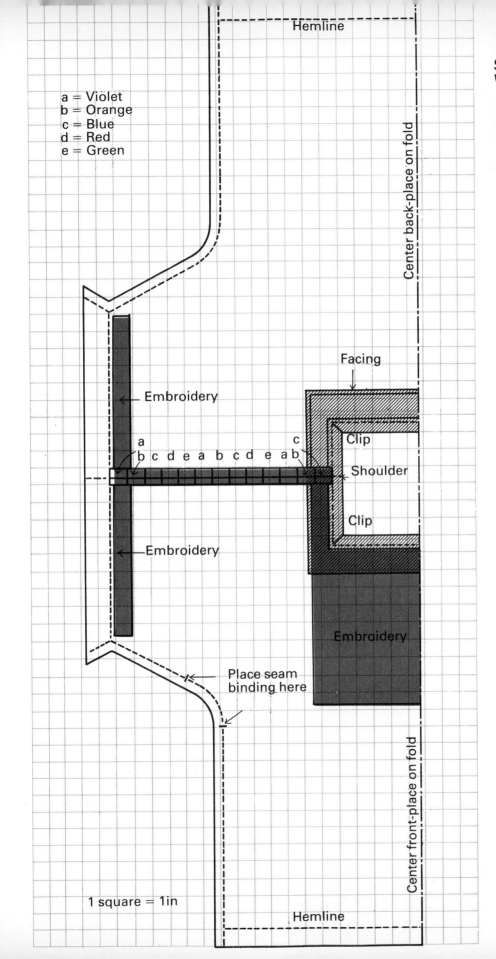

a = Violet
b = Orange
c = Blue
d = Red
e = Green

Hemline

Center back-place on fold

Facing

Embroidery

Clip

a
b c d e a b c d e a b
c

Shoulder

Clip

Embroidery

Embroidery

Place seam binding here

Center front-place on fold

1 square = 1in

Hemline

Special technique — Working a randa

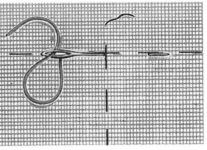

1. *Begin the randa at the shoulder neck edge. Starting with blue thread, bring the needle through the fabric ½in to the left of the basted shoulder line. Insert the needle at the shoulder line.*

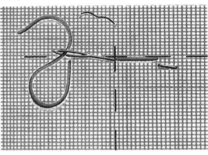

2. *Bring the needle out ½in to the right of the line, directly opposite the first stitch. Insert the needle again at the shoulder line, take it diagonally behind and bring it out just below the first stitch. Continue stitching the randa in this way.*

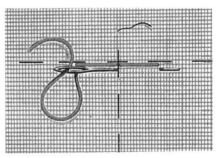

3. *Work for about 1in, then change color and repeat to form another 1in-long block. Continue to work different colored blocks down the entire length of the sleeve. Repeat on the other sleeve.*

1 square = 3 threads

Grecian doll

Stylized plant forms, birds and animals, and the Tree of Life are recurring themes in Greek embroidery and were interpreted in different techniques according to local tradition, distinguishing one group of islands from another. These rich and elaborate designs are simplified here to make bright-colored borders and unusual motifs for modern use, while retaining all the charm of the originals.

Size
To fit a 24in chest

You will need
1¾yd of 36in-wide (or 1½yd of 45in-wide) cotton poplin
1 skein each of pearl cotton in red, blue, yellow, green and brown
⅜yd of 36in-wide Penelope canvas, with 10 double threads to 1in
Tapestry needle
10in dress zipper
Sewing thread to match fabric
Dressmaker's graph paper
Tailor's chalk

Skills you need
Cross-stitch
Holbein stitch

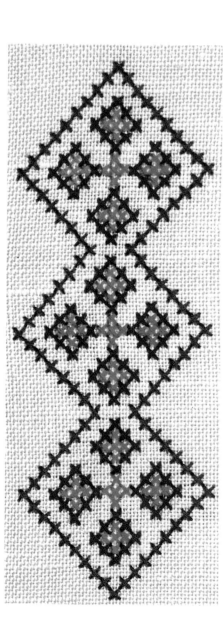

To prepare the work

Scale up the pattern pieces on page 87, using dressmaker's graph paper. Transfer arrows and cutting information. Cut out the pattern.

Press the fabric and lay it flat. Place the bodice front pattern piece on the fabric, aligning the arrow with the straight grain of the fabric, and pin in place. Draw around the cutting line with tailor's chalk, or mark the cutting line with basting stitches in a contrasting color. Repeat with the bodice back piece, reversing the pattern piece to obtain right and left sides. Mark the outline of the pocket. Mark the upper and lower fold lines with basting.

Remove pattern pieces and cut out marked areas as rectangles of fabric. Do not cut along cutting lines. Mark the center of the bodice front with basting stitches using a contrasting color thread.

Place a piece of Penelope canvas large enough to cover the whole of the bodice front on the right side of the front bodice piece, aligning the vertical canvas threads with the center front. Pin the canvas along the center front and then from the center horizontally out to the sides and diagonally to the top and bottom edges (see page 76). Baste and remove the pins.

To work the embroidery

Begin at the center front neckline, 1¼in below the cutting line and work the border from the center to each shoulder in turn. Work from the chart opposite. Be careful to work an equal distance from the cutting line marked on the cotton fabric, which should be visible through the canvas. Use 3 strands of floss throughout. Finish the border ⅝in from the cutting line at the shoulder seam.

Work the figures in the bustline border 1½in above the cutting line. Center the border around the center front and work from the center to each side in turn.

When the embroidery is completed, remove the basting holding the canvas about an inch from the edge of the embroidery. Ease out the canvas threads one by one as shown on page 76.

Repeat on the back bodice pieces and work the geometric border on the top of the pocket between upper and lower fold lines.

To make the dress

Once these four pieces have been embroidered and the canvas removed, cut out along the cutting lines marked on the fabric. Cut out the remaining pattern pieces for the skirt and for front and back facings in cotton poplin.

Place bodice front and front facing right sides together, and pin around the neck and armholes. Start and finish stitching ⅝in from the shoulder edge. Trim the seam allowance around the neck and armhole to ¼in and clip the curves. Turn right side out and press. Repeat with left and right bodice back pieces and facings.

Place bodice front and back pieces right sides together and pin along the shoulder seams. Stitch. Press the seams open. Turn under the seam allowances at the shoulder on the facings and slip stitch together.

With bodice front and back pieces right sides together, open out the facings at the sides and pin the side seams together on the bodice and facings. Stitch each side as one continuous seam. Press the seams open and turn the facings to the wrong side. Turn under the seam allowance on the bottom edge of the facing and press.

To make the pocket, turn the top to the wrong side along the fold line and then fold it back to the right side along the upper fold line to expose the border of embroidery. Turn under ¼in on the top edge and slip stitch to the wrong side of the pocket. Pin the folded fabric together at the sides of the pocket and baste along the upper and lower edges. Run a row of gathering stitches around the edge and pull them up to make a good curve, turning the seam allowance to the wrong side. Baste around the edge. Press the pocket. Pin, baste and stitch it in place on the skirt front.

Place the skirt back pieces right sides together and stitch the center back seam to the notch. Place front and back skirt pieces right sides together, and pin along the side seams. Stitch and press seams open.

Run two rows of gathering stitches along the top of the skirt pieces, keeping within the seam allowance. Pull up the gathers to fit the bodice.

Pin the skirt to the bodice, right sides together, matching side seams and adjusting the gathers evenly. Baste and stitch. Slip stitch the facing in place. Turn under the seam allowances on the center back seam and insert the zipper. Turn under the seam allowances on the facings and slip stitch along the zipper tape. Sew a hook and eye at the top. Hem the skirt.

↑Center

Dress pattern 1 square = 2in; ⅝in seam allowance included

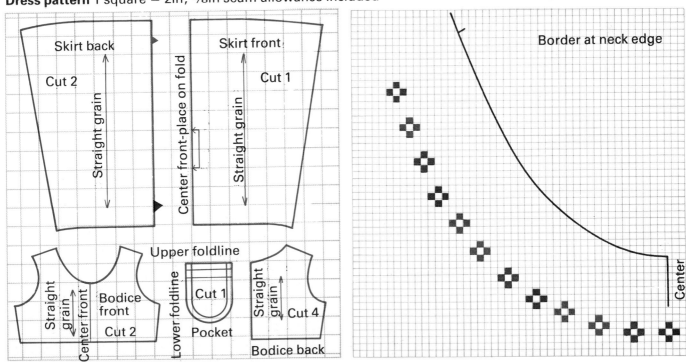

Skirt back
Cut 2
Straight grain

Center front-place on fold

Skirt front
Cut 1
Straight grain

Border at neck edge

Upper foldline

Straight grain
Center front
Bodice front
Cut 2

Lower foldline

Cut 1
Pocket

Straight grain
Cut 4
Bodice back

Center

87

Jolly juggler

Brighten a pair of overalls with this clever little juggling clown worked in cross-stitch.

Size
The motif measures 5¼in tall and 3¾in wide, but can be reduced or enlarged as described below.

You will need
A pair of children's overalls
1 skein each of stranded embroidery floss in red, white, black, yellow and green
Piece of Penelope canvas 6in square with 10 double threads to 1in
Tapestry needle
Hard pencil or canvas marker
Sewing needle and thread

To work the embroidery
Find the center of the bib by measuring up from the top of the waistband and across from the side of the bib and basting along these two lines.
Find the center of the canvas by measuring vertically and horizontally, and mark a cross where center pairs of threads intersect. (Be sure to mark the pairs of threads and not spaces between pairs.)
Place the canvas over the bib with the centers matching. Check that the upper and lower edges of the canvas are equi-distant from, and parallel to, the upper edge of the bib and the top of the waistband. Pin and baste the canvas in place around the edges (see page 76).
Using 6 strands of red floss in the tapestry needle, embroider the mouth, placing the center stitch over the vertical center pair of threads and the second horizontal pair above the center, as shown.

Work the rest of the design following the chart and using 6 strands of floss throughout.

To finish
When the embroidery is completed, saturate it with warm water. Gently pull out the canvas threads. Press the work on the wrong side.

To adjust the size of the motif
Use smaller or larger gauge canvas and fewer or more strands of thread. The clown would make an appealing decoration on curtains or window shades in a child's room. Work it as a patch pocket for a little girl's skirt, or use it to brighten up a drawstring bag for carrying dancing or gym clothes.

Henny Penny

"Wait for me" cries Chick Number Three as he sees Mother Hen and the other chicks scurrying away across the farmyard. Use the technique of cross-stitch over canvas to embroider this happy family group on children's clothes.

You will need
A piece of mono canvas 4 x 10in, with 5 threads to 1in
1 skein of stranded embroidery floss in each of the following colors: bright yellow, brown, tan, red and black
Dressmaker's carbon paper or felt-tip pens
Tapestry needle

To work the embroidery
Trace the outlines of the hen and chicks from the chart. Using dressmaker's carbon paper or colored pens, transfer the designs onto the canvas.
Pin and baste the canvas in place on the right side of the garment.
Using three strands of embroidery thread, follow the chart. Work one stitch over each thread of canvas (see page 76).
When the embroidery is completed, trim the excess canvas from the edges of the design. Strand by strand, pull the threads of the canvas from underneath the embroidery stitches.
Press on the wrong side.

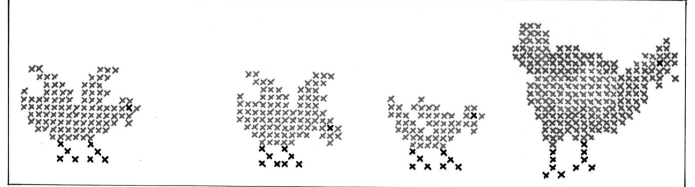

Ming vest

Blue and white are the traditional colors of the cross-stitch of rural China. The peasants embroidered simple garments for their children which they believed protected them. Work the symbols for prosperity and good fortune on a baby's vest.

Size

To fit a 22in chest
To make the vest one size larger, add 2½in all around (with a total of 5in on on the left side fold). To make it one size smaller, take off 2½in all around.

You will need

⅜yd of 36in-wide white evenweave cotton, with 28 threads to 1in
⅜yd of 45in-wide dark blue lightweight cotton
2 skeins of stranded embroidery floss in navy
Tapestry needle
Embroidery hoop
Paper for pattern
Sewing thread to match fabric

Skills you need

Cross-stitch
Holbein stitch

To work the embroidery

Following the chart on page 93, scale up the pattern and cut it out. Pin it to the white cotton, following the straight grain of the fabric. Baste around the outline of the garment in a contrasting color thread. Baste lines to indicate the center front, center back and left side. Remove the paper pattern. Using a tapestry needle and an embroidery hoop, start the embroidery at the center of the border (A) and work outward on both sides. Use two strands of floss and work over two threads. Position the rabbit by beginning at the center (B) about 3¼in above the bottom edge of the vest front. Next, embroider the butterflies (C) on the front and back of the vest, counting an equal number of threads on each side of the center front and center back to position them. The geometric wheel (D) and the peach (E) can then be centered between the butterflies, with the geometric wheel on the front and the peach on the back. Embroider the bats (G) and the double coins (F), counting the threads from the center front line. Press the completed embroidery on the wrong side.

To make the vest

Cut out the vest. Pin the paper pattern on the dark blue lining fabric and cut it out. Join the left shoulder seam of the vest to the lining. Place the lining inside the vest, with wrong sides together, and baste around the edges, taking a ⅜in seam allowance, which has been included.
To make the binding, cut bias strips 1½in wide from the blue fabric. Join the strips as necessary to make a continuous length. With right sides together, pin the binding around the edge of the vest, starting and finishing at the left shoulder. With the right side on top, stitch the binding in place, taking a ¼in seam. Fold the binding to the inside and slip stitch.
Make four Chinese buttons and loops from the blue fabric (see below) and stitch in place as shown on the pattern.
All the symbols on the vest are traditional good wishes.
A. 'Shou' character border signifies longevity. B. Rabbit wards off evil.
C. Butterfly signifies joy. D. Geometric wheel signifies good luck.
E. Peach is the fruit of life. F. Double coins signify prosperity.
G. Bat signifies happiness.

Special technique — Chinese ball buttons

1. *For each button, cut a strip of fabric 1in wide and 8in long. Fold in half lengthwise, with right sides together. Stitch, taking a ¼in seam allowance. Trim the seam close to the stitching. Turn the strip right side out, using a bodkin or blunt knitting needle.*

2. *To tie the knot, start at point A. Make two loops, one on top of the other. Thread the other end of the strip alternately over and under the loops to end at point B. Pull gently to tighten the knot. Trim the ends and slip stitch together, then sew the button to the garment.*

3. *To make a button loop for each button, cut a strip of fabric 1in wide and 3in long. Make a tube as shown in step 1. Fold the strip in half and slip stitch together along the seamlines, leaving a loop to slip over the button. Fold under the ends and sew the loop in place opposite the button.*

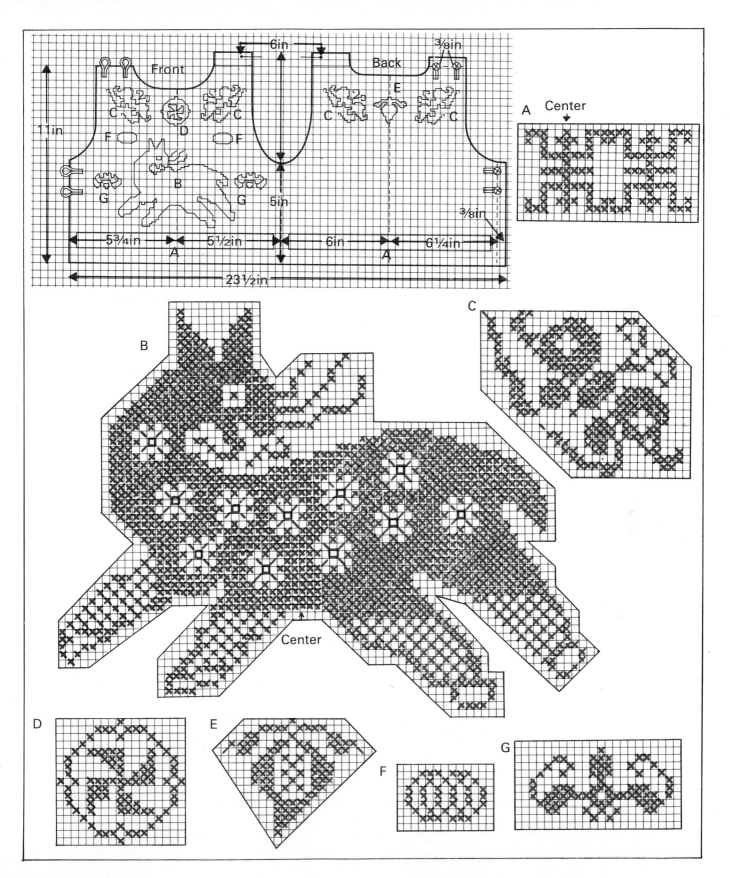

93

More design ideas

Guardian angels

A really special occasion, like the christening of a new baby, is enhanced by a special hand-embroidered gown that is sure to become a treasured family heirloom.

This christening gown has been given a special meaning with a hand-embroidered motif.

The ring of flowers is supported by hovering cherubs, and another angel is embroidered on the yoke of the gown. The sash is adorned with a delicate border of flowers and greenery. This pattern is repeated around the hem of the robe and underlined by a simple geometric motif. All the embroidery is worked in cross-stitch in pretty pastel shades. The floral ring is worked in blue and the flower border is pink to make the gown traditionally suitable for a boy or a girl, so you can get started long before the expected birth! The design can be adapted to use either on a ready-made gown, or on one you make yourself. The border of flowers could also be used to edge a tiny matching bonnet.

You will need
Christening gown made in evenweave fabric
Stranded embroidery floss in the following colors and quantities:
2 skeins each of medium pink and green; 1 skein each of light blue, medium blue, dark blue, turquoise, shell pink, dark pink, yellow, dark yellow
Crewel needle
Embroidery hoop (optional)

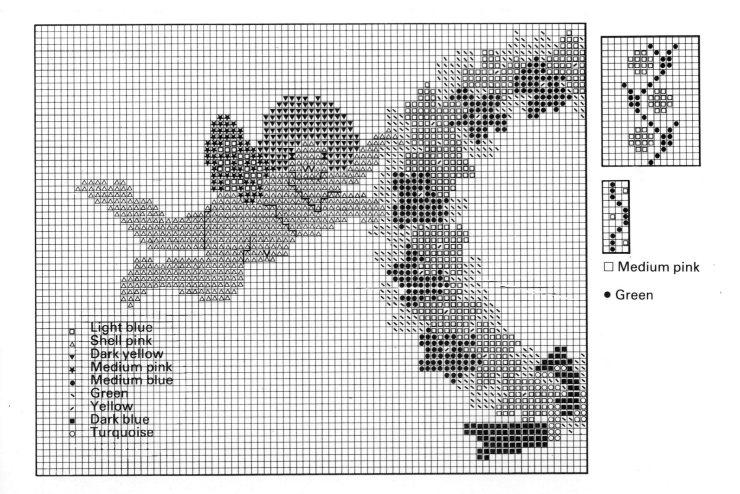

☐ Medium pink
● Green

- ☐ Light blue
- △ Shell pink
- ▼ Dark yellow
- ✳ Medium pink
- • Medium blue
- ＼ Green
- ، Yellow
- ■ Dark blue
- ○ Turquoise

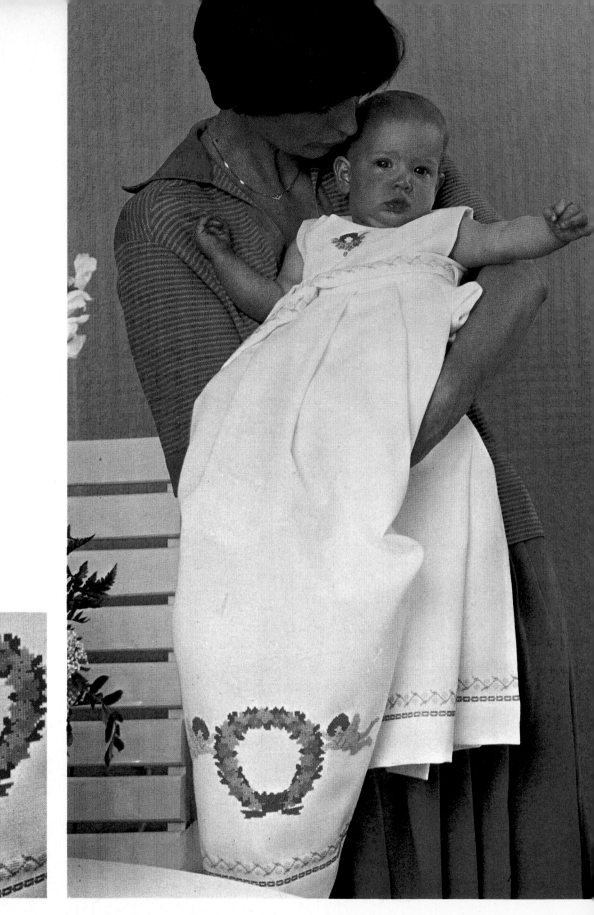

BAGS
AND
BELTS

Oriental satchel

This beautiful satchel, with a Star of Solomon design, is adapted from the saddle bags used by the Qashqā'i tribe of southern Persia. The design could be easily adapted to make a pillow, or you could alter the star to be used individually on a variety of useful and decorative items.

To prepare the canvas

Using either a line of basting or a waterproof marking pen, mark the center of the canvas lengthwise. Leave at least 3½in at the bottom for framing and stretching, and outline the area of the bag front. Leave a further 3½in above the front, and outline the bag flap.

Stretch the canvas in the frame or bind the raw edges with masking tape to prevent the canvas from raveling and the yarn from catching.

To work the embroidery

Mark the center of the canvas horizontally. Following the chart, begin with the center diamond. Working in cross-stitch and with a single strand of yarn throughout, embroider from the center outward, outlining the stars and diamonds first. Complete the fillings and the first dark blue line of the border. Work the next two rows in cross-stitch over a single intersection. Complete the border with a row of couching; three strands of yarn are couched with a single strand.

Work the animals on the flap in velvet stitch, working over a single intersection and using a single strand of yarn.

Fill in the background and work the border as before. Using small sharp-pointed scissors, cut the velvet stitch loops to give a carpet pile effect.

Remove the canvas from the frame and stretch if necessary.

To finish

Cut out the bag flap and front section, allowing a ¾in seam allowance all around. With right sides together, pin and baste the velvet backing to the flap and the bottom of the front section. Stitch with matching thread.

With right sides together, join the side seams in the same way. Trim the corners and seams.

Attach the beaded fringe as shown below. Make two ties, each 6in long, in

Size
8½ x 12¾in

You will need

½yd of 24in-wide mono canvas, 10 threads to 1in
Persian yarn in the following colors and quantities:
6 skeins dark blue; 4 skeins each bright blue, gray-blue, red; 2 skeins each pink, cream, bright yellow
Piece of dark red velvet, 10¼ x 13½in, for backing
Piece of dark red silk, 13½ x 21¾in, for lining
16 wooden beads in mixed colors
Tapestry needle
Scroll frame
Sewing thread to match fabric

Skills you need
Cross-stitch
Couching
Velvet stitch

Special technique —
Making a beaded fringe

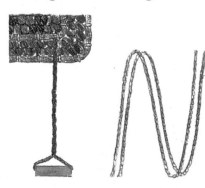  

1. First decide the depth of the finished fringe and multiply the measurement by three. Using two strands of yarn, cut the required lengths of yarn in a variety of colors. The exact number will depend on how full you wish the fringe to be.

2. Have ready a selection of beads in a variety of colors. Begin twisting the first length of yarn in the fingers. Twist until the yarn begins to curl back on itself. Loosen the twist, thread on a bead and re-twist the strand.

3. With the two ends of yarn in one hand and the bead in the other, pull gently. Let the bead go and shake firmly. Thread the loose ends into a large needle and take it through the bottom of the bag below the couched line. Knot ends of yarn together firmly. Repeat at regular intervals.

a similar way to the fringe and stitch in the places shown on the chart overleaf, as indicated by stars.

Fold the lining, right sides together, to make a similar bag shape and stitch the side seams. Press a ¾in allowance on the top edge of the pocket to the wrong side. With the right sides of the bag flap and the lining together, baste and stitch around the flap, leaving an opening. Turn right side out and press on the wrong side. Slip the lining into the bag, turn under the canvas seam on the top edge of the pocket to match the lining and slip stitch the two together. From the remaining yarn, except cream, cut lengths, each 90in long, and twist into a cord for the handle (see page 79). Slip stitch it in place along both side seams, placing the knotted ends at the bottom and extending them beyond the beads as tassels.

The color charts show a quarter of bag front and half of the flap.

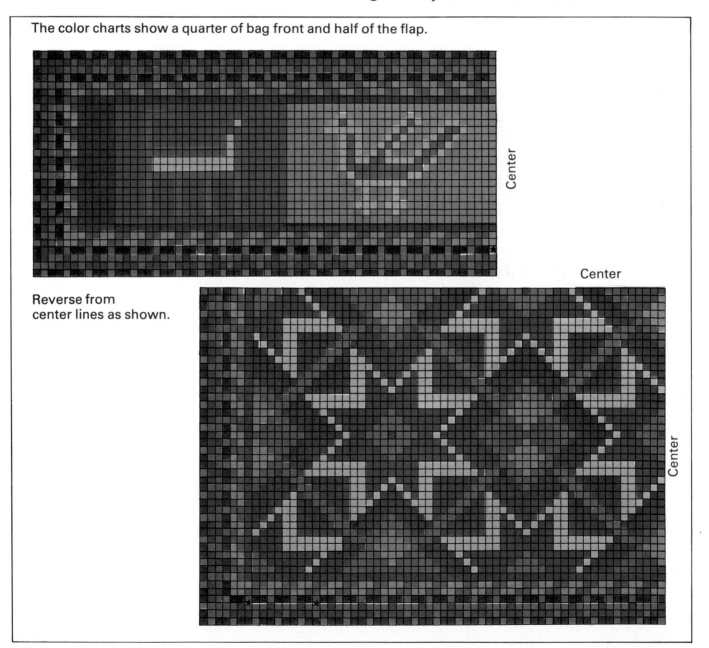

Reverse from center lines as shown.

Center

Center

Center

Rose evening purse

An evening purse, unlike its daytime counterpart, is not subject to the dictates of fashion—in one year and out the next. A beautiful evening bag can last a lifetime and still be handed down to become a family heirloom. A really beautiful bag can be very expensive, especially a handmade one, yet with a little time and patience and for a very small outlay, you can make your own.

Size
6½ x 7in

You will need
½yd of 36in-wide lightweight canvas, 14 threads to 1in
Crewel yarn in the following colors:
2 skeins each of dark pink, medium pink, light pink, shell pink, leaf green, olive green, light green, tan, medium brown, dark brown
16 skeins of black
Tapestry needle
Handbag frame 6½in wide at inner edges
⅜yd of 36in-wide non-woven interfacing
¼yd of lining fabric
Strong needle
Black button thread

Design and color
Careful thought should be given to design and color. For a lasting item you do not want the rage of the moment but one with an enduring quality. If it is to be your only evening purse, a careful mixture of colors which will go with any garment is essential.
The design shown here has been carefully chosen bearing these points in mind. For the background black is an ideal choice because it is both practical and versatile. While neutral colors such as beige or gray can be

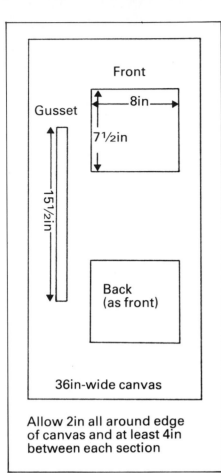

Front

Gusset

8in

7½in

15½in

Back
(as front)

36in-wide canvas

Allow 2in all around edge
of canvas and at least 4in
between each section

attractive and could well be substituted in this design, remember that a
beige bag can look dirty when worn with a white outfit, and light colors
show the dirt more easily than darker ones. While it is possible to have an
evening bag dry-cleaned, it can be expensive and it may be difficult to find
a specialist in your neighborhood.

Transferring the design

Trace the outline of the bag front and back and the gusset on the canvas
with a felt-tip pen, allowing a 4in space between each section. At least 2in
of canvas must be left around the area to be worked to allow for stretching
and cutting a seam allowance.
Note that the gusset piece is placed on a fold, or must be reversed and
doubled.

To work the embroidery

Find the center of each of the back and front pieces of the bag canvas.
Using two strands of yarn throughout, work the pattern outlines, following
the chart. Work the design in cross-stitch on both the front and back of the
bag.
Fill in the background and work the gusset in cross-stitch using two strands
of black yarn throughout.

To assemble the evening purse

Baste non-woven interfacing cut to the same size to the wrong side of each
piece and stitch firmly around the edges.
Trim the interfacing and canvas to within ½in of the stitches all around.
Clip the seam allowance of the long edges of the gusset strip at ½in inter-
vals, to enable the gusset to be eased around the curves of the front and
back pieces.
Match the center of the gusset to the bottom center of one side of the purse,
right sides together. Pin, baste and sew firmly in place with backstitch.
Sew the other side of the purse to the gusset in the same way.
Cut V-shape notches in the seam allowances of the back and front, at ½in
intervals to reduce bulk if necessary.
Turn right side out and turn in the seam allowance along the top edge.
Insert the top edges into the purse frame and hold them in place with pins
pushed through the holes in the frame.
Attach the purse to the frame by sewing through the holes in the frame and
through the fabric with a strong needle and black button thread.
To make the lining, cut two pieces of lining fabric 7in by 7½in, and cut a
strip 2in wide by 19in long for the gusset. These measurements include
½in seam allowances all around. Assemble the lining as for the purse.
Place lining in the purse, wrong sides together. Turn under the top edges
of the lining and slip stitch in place to the canvas seam allowance just below
the frame, and to meet the embroidery at the gusset edges.

To adjust the size

To change the size of the pattern to make a different item, see page 9.

center

Top

Design shown actual size

Light-hearted tote

A multitude of uses for this tote bag make it the ideal gift, although you will be tempted to make it for carrying your own needlework. A scattering of flowers and leaves worked in vibrant colors around the central heart gives a pleasantly haphazard effect. Vary the colors and the arrangement of the design to suit your taste—look through your collection of left-over knitting yarn to see if you can use materials that are already on hand.

To work the embroidery
Each side of the bag is worked separately, using two strands of knitting worsted over two double threads of canvas in each direction. Find the center of the canvas and mark it with pencil or a line of basting stitches. Work the design from the center outward. Remember to allow at least 2in all around the worked area for blocking. Follow the chart opposite for placement of colors.

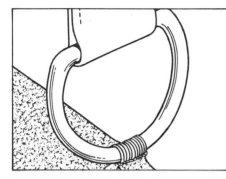

You can if you wish paint the canvas with acrylic paints before the design has been worked, to prevent any of the canvas from showing through the yarn when worked. Block the completed canvas.

Assembling the bag

Trim the canvas to within ⅝in of the worked area. With right sides together, baste and stitch each piece (front and back) to the wool lining fabric. Leave the bottom edge open; turn right side out. Insert a piece of doweling along the top edge of each piece, holding it in place with a second line of stitching. Close the bottom (fourth) side by hand on the right side, since it is the least prominent of the four seams and will be on the inside of the completed bag.

To make the gusset, cut a strip of wool fabric 5in by 42in. Fold lengthwise and stitch all around, leaving a 2in opening so that the strip can be turned right side out. Slip stitch the opening closed and press. Using Cretan stitch, sew the gusset to the sides of the bag. Work from the inside, starting and finishing with the ends of the gusset about 2in below the top edge of the bag.

To make the handles, cut two strips of wool lining fabric, each 3½ by 20in. Baste a strip of interfacing in place on each piece and fold lengthwise, right sides together. Baste and stitch along the length of the strip. Turn each strip right side out and close both ends. For extra strength and durability, top-stitch the handles around all edges. Place the D-rings on the top edge of the bag about 5in from each corner and sew them in place with buttonhole stitch. Thread the ends of the handles through the rings and stitch the ends with strong thread to match fabric (see diagram opposite).

Size
13 x 20in

You will need
¾yd of 36in-wide Penelope canvas,
7 double threads to 1in
Knitting worsted in the following colors:
10oz dark pink, 1oz medium pink,
1oz pale pink, 2oz burnt orange, 1oz white and 1oz violet
1 skein each of pearl cotton in white and violet
Large tapestry needle or rug needle
1¼yds of 45in-wide wool fabric for lining, gusset and handles
2 pieces of ¼in doweling, 20in long
4 metal D-rings
2 pieces of non-woven interfacing, each 1¼ x 18in
Sewing thread to match fabric

•	white
o	violet
X	burnt orange
-	pale pink
/	medium pink
	background deep pink

Star-crossed tote

This richly decorated tote bag is worked in tapestry yarn with touches of synthetic raffia.

Size
7½ x 9in (plus handle)

You will need
½yd of 36in-wide mono canvas, 18 threads to 1in
Tapestry yarn in the following colors and quantities: 2 skeins each of dark blue, medium blue, green, pink, turquoise, lime green; 4 skeins of light blue; 20 skeins of purple
2 skeins of purple synthetic raffia
Tapestry needle
½yd of 36in-wide lining material
Sewing thread to match fabric

Skills you need
Cross-stitch
Double cross-stitch
Rice stitch
Diagonal satin stitch

Turning a corner with diagonal satin stitch

To use the pattern
Following the diagram, draw the outline of the bag on strong paper and cut it out. Baste the pattern to the canvas, leaving plenty of space around the shape for a ⅝in seam allowance and stretching. Also make sure that the grain line on the pattern follows the grain of the canvas.
Draw around the pattern using a felt-tipped pen, or mark it with basting. Remove the pattern and repeat to make the other side of the bag.
If you prefer, work only one side of the bag in canvas, using a textured fabric such as tweed for the second side. In this case, halve the amounts of yarn required.

To work the embroidery
Mark the center of each side with lines of basting, and plan the design out from the center. Following the chart, work the design on both sides of the bag.

To finish
When the work is completed, block and trim the canvas and cut out two pieces of lining the same shape as the trimmed canvas.
Pin and baste the two sides of the bag together, right sides facing, stitch from A to B (see diagram) using one of the seaming methods shown; then stitch the seam of the handle (see diagram).
Clip into the seam allowance on the curves, and turn the bag right side out. Fold back the seam allowance around the upper edge of the bag and handle edges and baste in place.
Sew the lining pieces together in the same way as for the bag, folding the seam allowance around the top and along the handle to the back, and then basting in place. Slip the lining into the bag, matching the seams to those of the bag. Pin, baste and slip stitch in place. Bring the lining right up to the edge of the embroidery so that no canvas is visible on the finished bag.

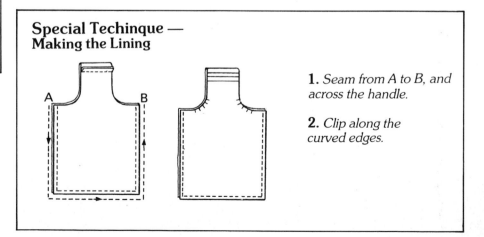

Special Techinque — Making the Lining

1. *Seam from A to B, and across the handle.*

2. *Clip along the curved edges.*

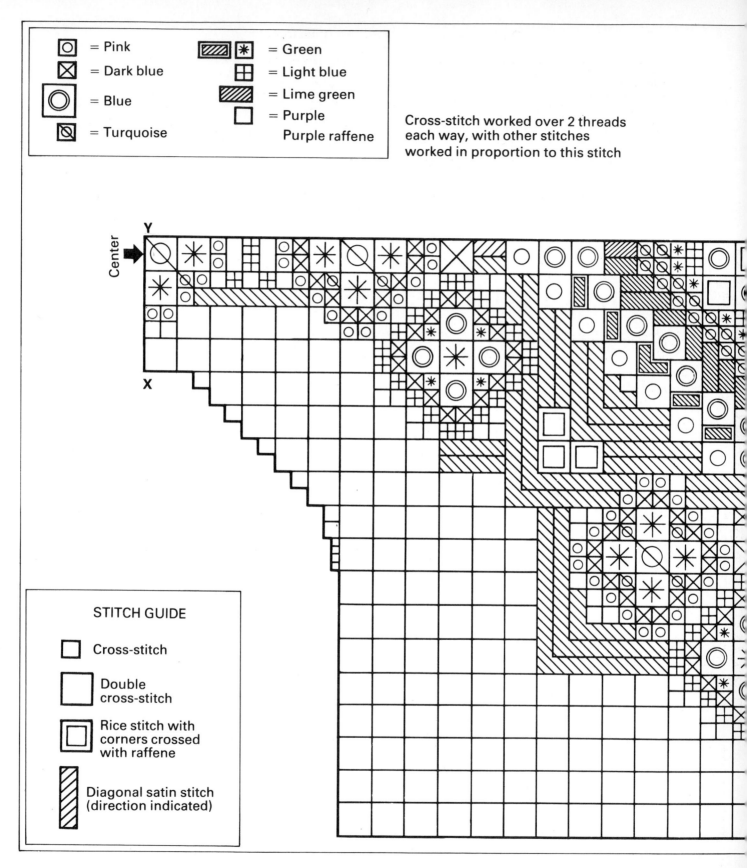

= Pink

= Dark blue

= Blue

= Turquoise

= Green

= Light blue

= Lime green

= Purple

Purple raffene

Cross-stitch worked over 2 threads each way, with other stitches worked in proportion to this stitch

Center

Y

X

STITCH GUIDE

Cross-stitch

Double cross-stitch

Rice stitch with corners crossed with raffene

Diagonal satin stitch (direction indicated)

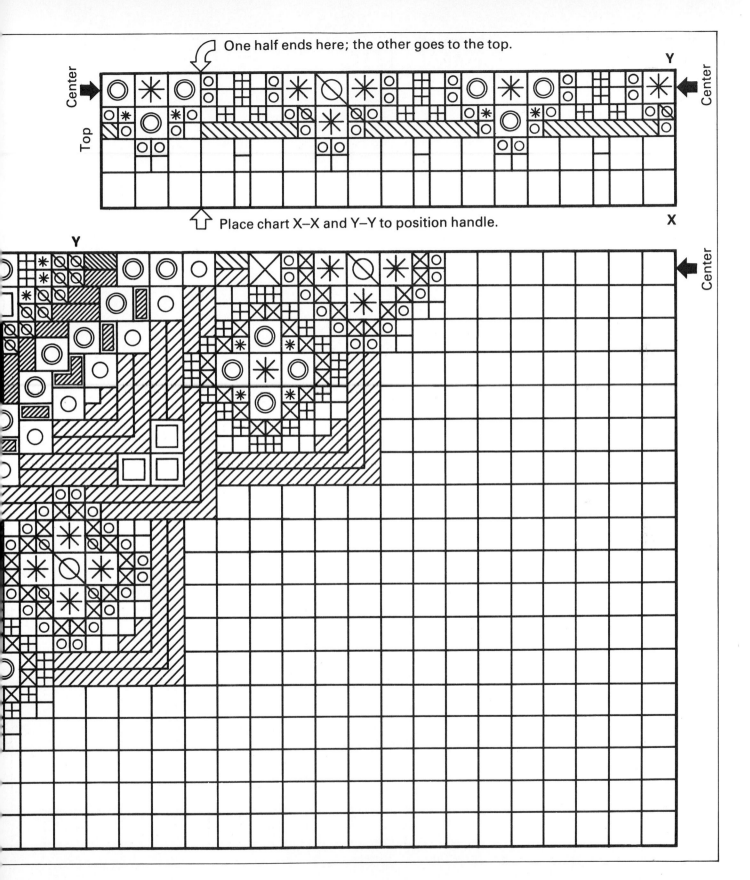

One half ends here; the other goes to the top.

Center ➤ Top

Place chart X–X and Y–Y to position handle.

Y

Center ➤

Y

109

Belting away

Despite its simplicity, cross-stitch is extremely effective and adaptable. These patterns all make marvellous belts and borders. Experiment with color schemes; a design worked in one color combination will look entirely different in another.

You will need
To work a design about two-thirds of the size of the ones shown here, use Penelope canvas with 14 double threads to 1in and tapestry yarn, stranded floss, or matte embroidery cotton. You can adapt designs to coarser or finer canvas, or to evenweave fabric, using appropriately thicker or thinner yarns or threads.

Skills you need
Cross-stitch
Half cross-stitch

Squares
This is a simple pattern using square motifs in three colors. Try using three shades of one color or use a black background with gray and white centers for a checkerboard look. For an all-over design for a pillow or tote bag, the square motifs could be grouped to form geometric patterns, or devise an interesting use of color against a contrasting background shade to achieve a fascinating patchwork effect.

Clover leaf
Use half cross-stitch or cross-stitch for this pretty design. If you work the design in a different combination of subtle colors, the whole character of the design becomes more sophisticated. To add more texture, work the background in cross-stitch and the clover leaves in half cross-stitch.

Diamonds

This design lends itself to being repeated over a large area and can readily be adapted for a cummerbund, bag, stool top, or chair seat. Or, make an exotic vest in gold, copper and silver metallic thread on evenweave cotton or linen.

To get a completely different effect, turn the design so that the small center squares become diamonds, and the outline diamonds become squares.

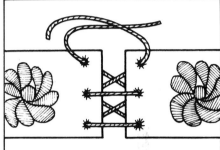

Work eyelets on each end of a tie belt and thread with a matching cord.

Design ideas

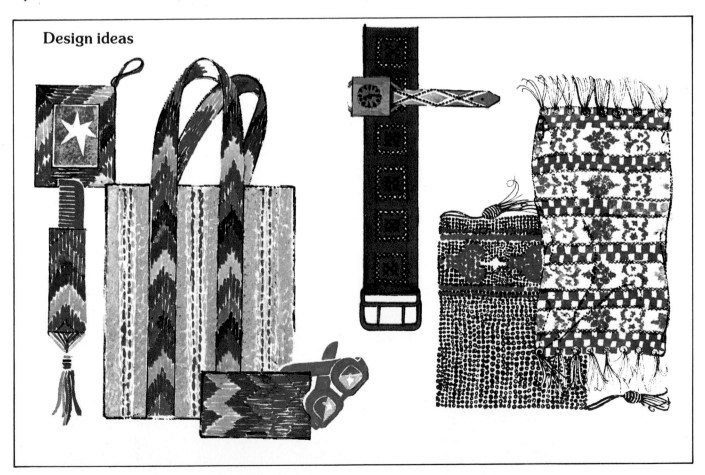

Butterflies alight

An ever-popular motif for children and adults alike is the butterfly—and it's easy to see why. They add color to everything they alight on and are entirely adaptable to evenweave embroidery fabric or canvas. Vary the color combinations and you discover that the possibilities are almost limitless.

You will need
¼yd of 36in-wide lightweight canvas, 16 threads to 1in (This should be enough to allow ample seam allowances on the finished belt.)
Tapestry yarn in the following colors:
1 skein each bright green, bright red, leaf green, red-orange, deep red, bright yellow
1–2 skeins of white, depending on waist measurement
Tapestry needle
Interfacing cut to waist measurement x 6in
¼yd of 36in-wide backing fabric

Skills you need
Cross-stitch
Eyelet stitch

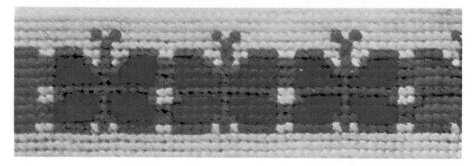

The simpler of these two butterflies is easy enough for a child to work, perhaps as a bookmark or belt. The waist-cinching tie-belt is an obvious choice for more experienced needleworkers. If you put your mind to the possibilities for adapting this design, there is no end to the number of places these butterflies are likely to land.

Special technique — Making a belt

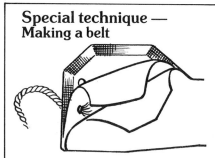

Fold the excess canvas to the back of the work and interline with iron-on interfacing to give the belt some body. Cut out the lining from the backing fabric, leaving a ½in seam allowance all around. Turn under the allowance and slip stitch the lining in place.

To work the embroidery
Work the large butterfly on the front and work a border of small butterflies all around.
Any length belt can be worked, but placing the small butterfly motifs must be done very carefully. It is best to start from the center back of the belt and to work around to the front, leaving enough space between the last small

butterfly and the larger design to prevent overcrowding the design. Either place the center of the first small motif directly on the center back line, or position the small butterflies so that center back line comes directly between two of them.

To make the belt
Cut away the excess canvas leaving about $\frac{1}{2}$in all around the worked area of the belt for seam allowances. Using this as a pattern, cut out a piece of backing fabric the same size. Fold the excess canvas to the back of the work. Cut a piece of interfacing to this size. With wrong sides together, baste the interfacing to the backing fabric and baste down the seam allowances on the wrong side. With wrong sides together, slip stitch the belt to the interfaced backing fabric.

If possible, punch the eyelet holes and bind them with metal eyes. Eyelets can be worked using eyelet stitch worked in pearl cotton. Eyelets should always be worked in cotton thread which is far stronger than wool yarn. A larger, stronger central hole can be formed.

Other ways to use this design
The small butterflies make a charming design for a small pillow; they can be placed to form a circle or scattered at random and worked in cotton or yarn on evenweave fabric or canvas.

These tiny motifs also look charming individually or in pairs on a blouse, a dress or a child's pinafore.

Enlarge a single large butterfly and use it for a child-size shoulder bag with a braided strap or on a scarf or a pocket.

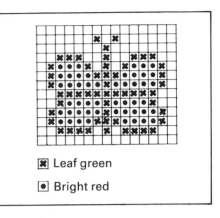

☒ Leaf green

⊡ Bright red

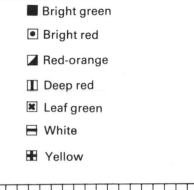

■ Bright green

⊡ Bright red

◪ Red-orange

Ⅲ Deep red

☒ Leaf green

⊟ White

⊞ Yellow

Elegance at hand

Quick-make accessories make you feel special, or work one for a friend. There are two charming designs to wear as belt or shoe buckles, and two watchband designs, one striped and one patterned with rosebuds.

Oval buckle

Size
2 x 2¾in

You will need
6in square of Penelope canvas, 10 double threads to 1in
1 skein of tapestry yarn in each of the following colors: cerise, orange, dark red, purple, cyclamen pink, rose pink, blood red, lilac
Tapestry needle
Small square of heavy cardboard
Small piece of ¼in-thick foam padding
Small piece of backing fabric
Button thread

Butterfly buckle

Size
2⅜ x 2¾in

You will need
6in square of Penelope canvas, 16 double threads to 1in
Stranded embroidery floss: 1 skein each of dark red, orange, dark brown, light brown, blue, light pink, dark pink, lilac, cream
Tapestry needle
Small piece of heavy cardboard
Small piece of ¼in-thick foam padding
Small piece of backing fabric
Sewing thread to match fabric
Button thread

To work the oval buckle
Work the design in cross-stitch following the chart overleaf. Using two strands of yarn, work each stitch over two threads.

To work the butterfly buckle
Using four strands of floss, work the design in cross-stitch following the chart. When the embroidery is complete, block the canvas lightly.

To make the buckles
Cut a piece of cardboard slightly smaller than the area of worked canvas. Glue a piece of foam padding to the cardboard and trim it to the same shape. Stretch the embroidery over the middle of the cardboard and lace it firmly in place using button thread.
To cover the back of the buckle neatly, cut a piece of backing fabric to the same shape as the buckle, allowing ½in all around for seam allowances. Turn the edges under and press down. With wrong sides together, slip stitch the backing to the buckle using matching thread.

114

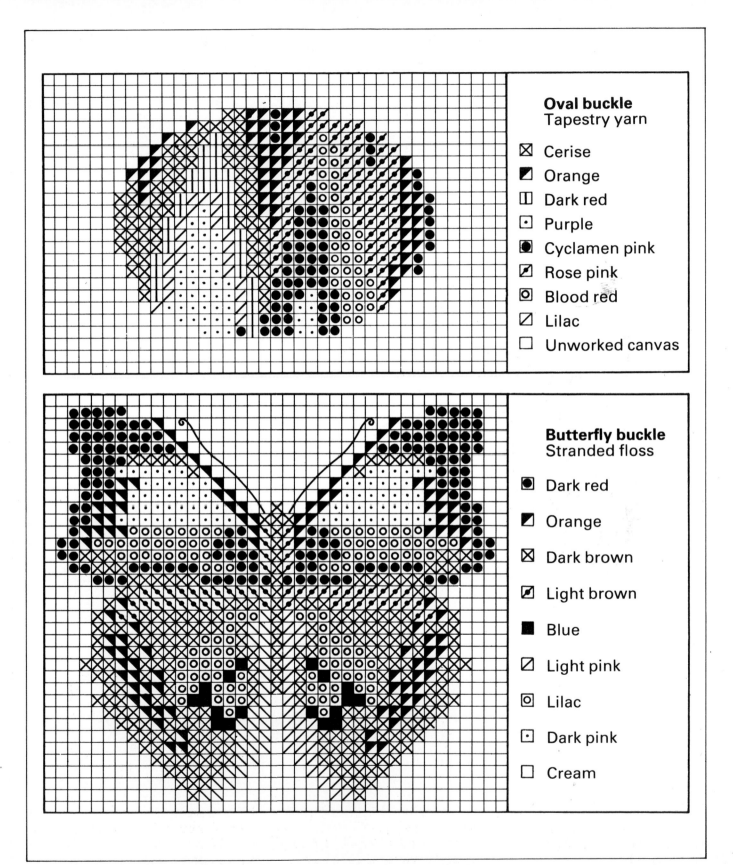

Oval buckle
Tapestry yarn

⊠ Cerise

◪ Orange

⊞ Dark red

⊡ Purple

● Cyclamen pink

◪ Rose pink

◉ Blood red

◪ Lilac

☐ Unworked canvas

Butterfly buckle
Stranded floss

● Dark red

◪ Orange

⊠ Dark brown

◪ Light brown

■ Blue

◪ Light pink

◉ Lilac

⊡ Dark pink

☐ Cream

Rosebud watchband

You will need
Small strip of mono canvas, 18 threads to 1in
1 skein of stranded embroidery floss in each of the following colors: light green, olive green, light pink, cerise, bright green
Tapestry needle
¾in-wide grosgrain or satin ribbon for backing
Buckle for fastening
Sewing thread to match ribbon

Skills you need
Cross-stitch
Eyelet stitch

Striped watchband

You will need
Small strip of Penelope canvas, 10 double threads to 1in
1 skein of tapestry yarn in each of the following colors: bright red, rose pink, cyclamen
Tapestry needle
½in-wide grosgrain or satin ribbon for backing
Buckle for fastening
Sewing thread to match ribbon

Skills you need
Cross-stitch
Eyelet stitch

To work the rosebud watchband
Using two strands of floss, work the embroidery in cross-stitch over one thread, following the chart overleaf and repeating the pattern as necessary to achieve the desired length.

To work the striped watchband
Using two strands of yarn, work in rows of cross-stitch. Work one leg of the cross to the end of a row in the appropriate color; then work the other leg back in the opposite direction.

To make the watchbands
Trim canvas to remove as much thickness as possible, but leave about ¼in all around. Turn excess under and press down lightly. Cut a piece of ribbon to the finished length of the embroidery and slip stitch, wrong sides together, along the two long sides and one short end. Position the bar of the buckle across the open end and sew in place, enclosing the raw edges. Slip the strap through the watch body. Try it on and mark position of 3 eyelet holes.
Make eyelets by hand, using pearl cotton to match the background.

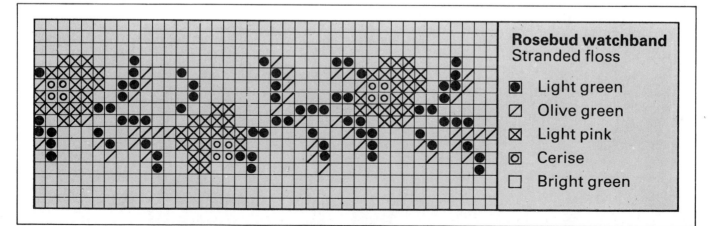

Rosebud watchband
Stranded floss

- ◉ Light green
- ⊘ Olive green
- ⊠ Light pink
- ◎ Cerise
- ☐ Bright green

GIFTS
TO MAKE
AND GIVE

Sweet scents

Work this lovely sachet with heart and snowflake motifs and a pretty tasseled drawstring for old-fashioned style.

Size
4³⁄₄ x 6¹⁄₄in

You will need
Piece of evenweave linen 15 x 20in, 26 threads to 1in
Stranded embroidery floss: 1 skein each light blue and dark blue
Tapestry needle
Crewel needle
Embroidery hoop
Basting thread
Scrap of white cotton fabric
Potpourri

Skills you need
Cross-stitch
Hemstitching

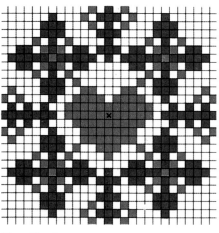

X = Center

To work the cross-stitch
Turn under the raw edges all around the linen and baste in place before framing on a straight-sided frame. Mark the central area as shown in the diagram using contrasting basting thread. Mark the center of one 4 x 5in rectangle and work the cross-stitch design in the center, following the diagram and using the tapestry needle and two strands of floss. Make sure all the top threads on the stitches cross each other in the same direction.

To work the hemstitching
Remove linen from frame. Pull out ten threads of the fabric ³⁄₄in above the top of the embroidery and keep the threads for stitching. Hemstitch the lower edge of the drawn threads, using the linen thread that was removed and working each stitch over two threads (see page 39).

To make the sachet bag
Measure a length of stranded embroidery floss six times as long as the final length required for the drawstring and make a twisted cord (see page 79). Thread the cord through the hemstitching and make tassels at each end. Make a small pouch from white cotton to fit inside the sachet bag. Fill it with dried lavender or potpourri and slip it into the embroidered bag.
Pull up the drawstring to close.

Other ways to use the design
The design could be adapted to make a jewelry bag for traveling, or to make a compact or lighter case.

On key

This pretty key ring is embroidered in cross-stitch with a colorful flower motif.

To work the embroidery

Following the chart (and the photograph for color), work the embroidery in the center of the linen, using three strands of embroidery floss throughout. Work in cross-stitch and use straight stitch for seams at lower corners, working each stitch over two threads of fabric. Press on the wrong side.

To make the key ring

Center the clear plastic circle on the right side of the embroidery. Cut away the excess linen from around the plastic circle. Place the plastic-covered embroidery on the circle of interfacing, then place these on the wrong side of the printed fabric circle. Baste edges to hold all the pieces together.
Place the bias fabric strip right side down on the plastic side of the circle, matching edges. Baste in place. To finish the ends, cut off excess and stitch the short ends together to fit. Stitch the strip in place, ¼in from the edge.
From the excess bias strip make a loop. Fold the strip in half lengthwise, right sides together. Pin, baste and stitch down the length, taking a ¼in seam. Turn the strip right side out and fold in half to form a loop. Sew the loop securely to the back of the circle at the center top, with raw edges matching and the loop lying inward. Turn bias strip over edge of circle to wrong side. Turn in ¼in on raw edge. Sew in place.
Fold loop upward, so that it lies flat against the circle and extends above it. Sew in place. Thread a key ring through the fabric loop.

Size

3¼in in diameter

You will need

4in square of evenweave linen, 22 threads to 1in
Stranded embroidery floss in light and dark pink, light and dark green, orange, mauve and rust
Tapestry needle
3¼in diameter circle of floral print cotton fabric and a 16 x 1¼in bias strip in the same fabric
3¼in diameter circle of clear plastic
3¼in diameter circle of heavyweight interfacing
Sewing thread to match linen
Sewing needle
Metal key ring

Skills you need

Cross-stitch
Straight stitch

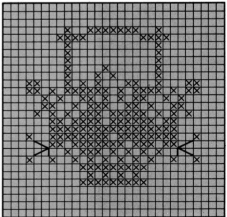

Eskimo slippers

The bold, multi-colored geometric patterns of Eskimo designs are traditionally executed in tiny squares of colored leather. They can be adapted to make striking borders worked in bright-colored cross-stitch.

Note

Work the band of embroidery on a firmly-woven cotton fabric. Avoid cotton twills or anything with a diagonal weave as it will be difficult to keep the embroidery straight. Work in matte embroidery cotton to give a solid look to each stitch, pearl cotton for a shiny finish, or stranded embroidery floss for small stitches in a more delicate border. Use tapestry or crewel yarn for a more textured look.

Use shirt suede for the slippers. This is slightly stretchy and thin and supple enough to be sewn by machine.

Or you can use felt or a strong cotton fabric such as denim or sailcloth. If you use fabric, you can work the embroidery directly onto the cloth instead of making a separate band of embroidery.

To cut out the slippers

Make a pattern on graph paper to fit a child's foot as shown below. Check the suede for any flaws or marks, and mark them on the wrong side with pencil or tailor's chalk. Lay the suede right side down on a flat, clean surface, and mark the pattern pieces, avoiding any marked flaws. Cut two left sides and two right sides for the upper slippers, and two strips to line the bands of embroidery. Cut two soles from the leather.

Cut four slipper sides (two right and two left), two soles, and two strips for the embroidery from the white cotton fabric. Allow extra fabric on the two strips for framing.

Size

To fit a child up to age 6

You will need

Piece of shirt suede 30in square
Piece of leather 10in square
½yd of 36in-wide white evenweave cotton
Matte embroidery cotton in the following colors and quantities: 1 skein each of green, yellow and black
2 skeins each of blue and red
Tapestry needle
Embroidery hoop
Sewing thread to match fabric
Graph paper
Sharp scissors
Soft pencil or tailor's chalk

Special technique — Making a pattern

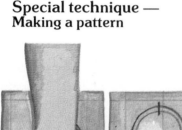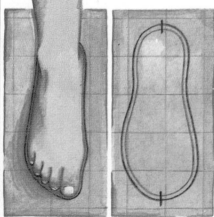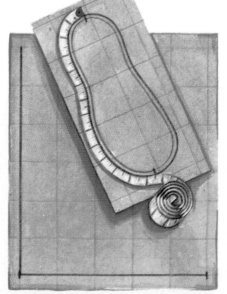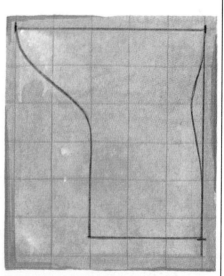

1. To make a pattern for a slipper, stand on a piece of graph paper and draw around the sole of the foot. Draw a second line ¾in outside of the first line and mark the center back and front.

2. Measure the sole from center back to center front and draw a horizontal line to this measurement on another piece of graph paper. This will be the bottom of the side pattern piece. Draw a vertical line at one end.

3. Measure the required height, allowing for seams and cuffs and mark them on pattern. Measure around leg at calf, divide by half and add 2¼in. Draw in this measurement as the width at top of pattern. Shape foot as shown.

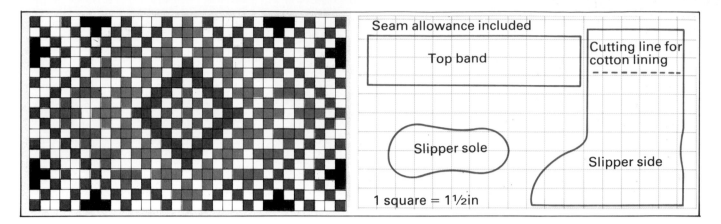

Seam allowance included

Top band

Cutting line for cotton lining

Slipper sole

Slipper side

1 square = 1½in

To work the embroidery

Work the cross-stitch on a scroll frame either by counting threads or by marking the center with tailor's chalk or lines of basting and working by eye. Follow the chart on page 123 for color sequence.

To finish

When the embroidery is completed, join the bands at the center backs and turn right side out. Turn under the edges to within ⅛in of the embroidery and baste in place.

Stitch the suede bands at the center back seams. The suede should be lightweight enough to stitch on the machine using an ordinary foot and a sharp needle. Place tissue paper under the suede when sewing to prevent the feed dog from marking the suede. Some sewing machines have a special leather foot which can also be used.

More design ideas

Work a border design on a large piece of burlap to make an unusual blotter, and attach small leather corners to hold the blotting paper. Work embroidered bands as details on the cuffs of a blouse or the sash of a dress, or decorate the edges of linen place mats or the corners of napkins.

Turn the bands right side out and slip the embroidered bands over them. Baste the embroidery to the center of the suede band and stitch along both edges. Remove basting.

Place the right and left sides, right side together, and stitch ⅛in from the edges at the center front and center back. Clip the curves. Pin the bottom edge to the leather soles and stitch ⅛in from the edges. Turn right side out. Make the cotton slipper liners in the same way, leaving ⅜in seam allowance.

Join the embroidered bands to the top of the slippers, right sides together. Turn the band to inside. Slip the cotton liners inside the slippers. Slip stitch the edge of the suede band to the cotton slipper liners and fold over the bands to expose the embroidery around the top of the slipper.

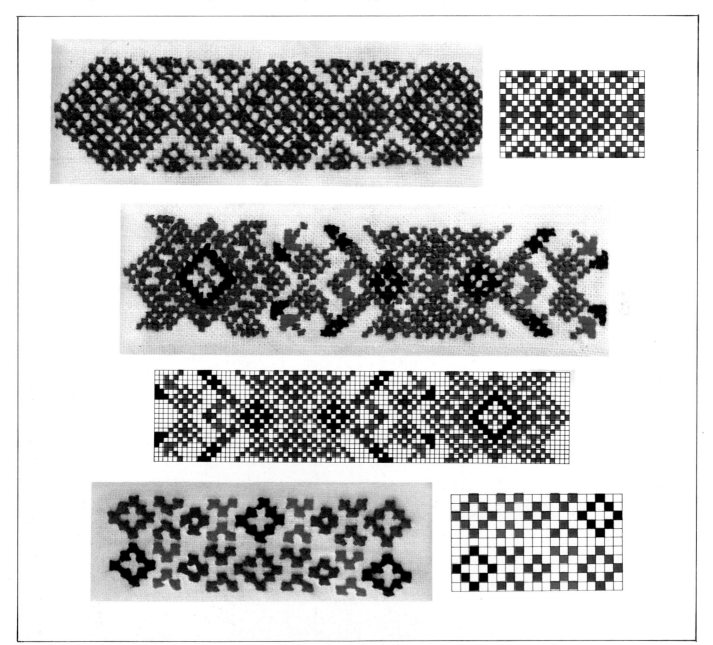

Happy ladybug

A ladybug coin purse worked in rich colors will keep loose change together.

Size
4½ x 6in

You will need
Piece of canvas 8 x 10in with 16 threads to 1in
Lining fabric 8 x 10in
Interfacing 7 x 9in
Coin purse frame
Crewel yarn in the following colors and quantities: 2 skeins each of royal blue, cherry red, fuchsia
3 skeins of white
Tapestry needle
Button thread to match fabric

To work the embroidery
The embroidery is worked in cross-stitch over two threads of canvas. Use three strands of yarn in the needle. Mark the center of the canvas in each direction. Fold the canvas in half widthwise, and mark the shape of the metal frame on both sides of the canvas.
Begin at the center and work outward to make the first row of the pattern. Complete the pattern by working one row below another. Work in one piece, reversing the design for the other side.

To finish
Stretch and finish with interfacing. Line the purse, leaving the top edges open. Turn right side out and slip stitch the edges together. Overcast the purse to the frame with strong button thread through the punched holes in the frame.

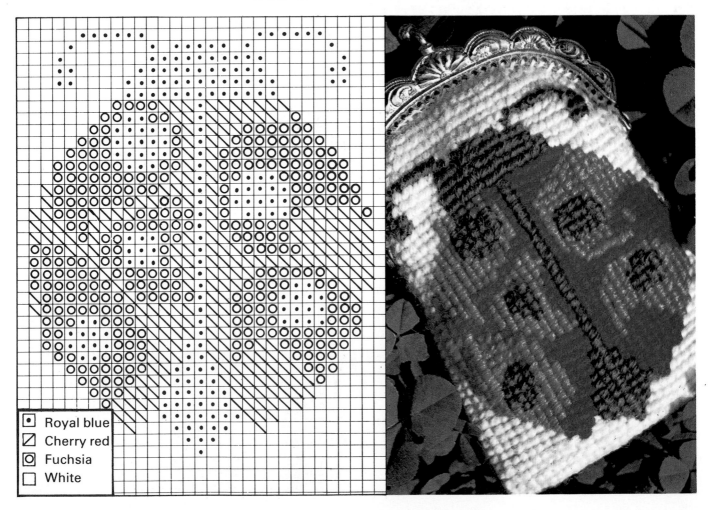

·	Royal blue
⧄	Cherry red
⊙	Fuchsia
☐	White

All change in linen

This coin purse has a snowflake motif on both sides, and the owner's name or initials can be worked on the inside pocket.

Size

4 x 6½in (open flat) with a pocket 2½in deep

You will need

Piece of evenweave linen 8 x 10in with 19 threads to 1in
1 skein each of stranded embroidery floss in scarlet and ruby red
Tapestry needle
Piece of lining fabric 5 x 7½in to match embroidery floss
Graph paper
Sewing thread to match fabric
Sewing needle

To work the embroidery

Work out your design on graph paper, with each square representing one stitch. Position your design on front and back of purse. Each cross-stitch is worked over two threads of linen using 3 strands of floss.
Work a border all around. The pocket can have a name or monogram worked on it if desired, and a border can be worked across the top.

To finish

When the embroidery is completed, cut out the purse, allowing seams of ½in all around beyond the border. Cut lining the same size.
With right sides together, stitch purse to lining, leaving an opening for turning. Do not to catch stitches in seam. Turn right out, slip stitch opening to close. Press lightly. Slip stitch pocket sides together, matching notches.

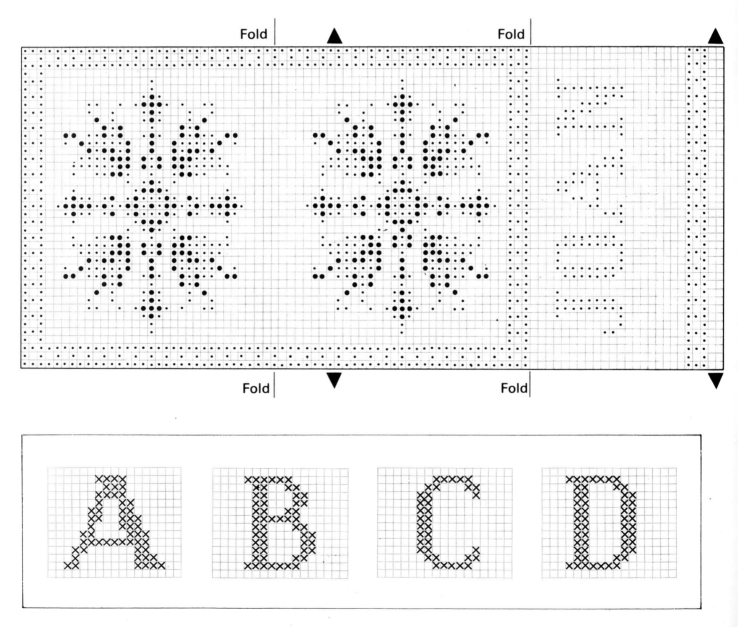

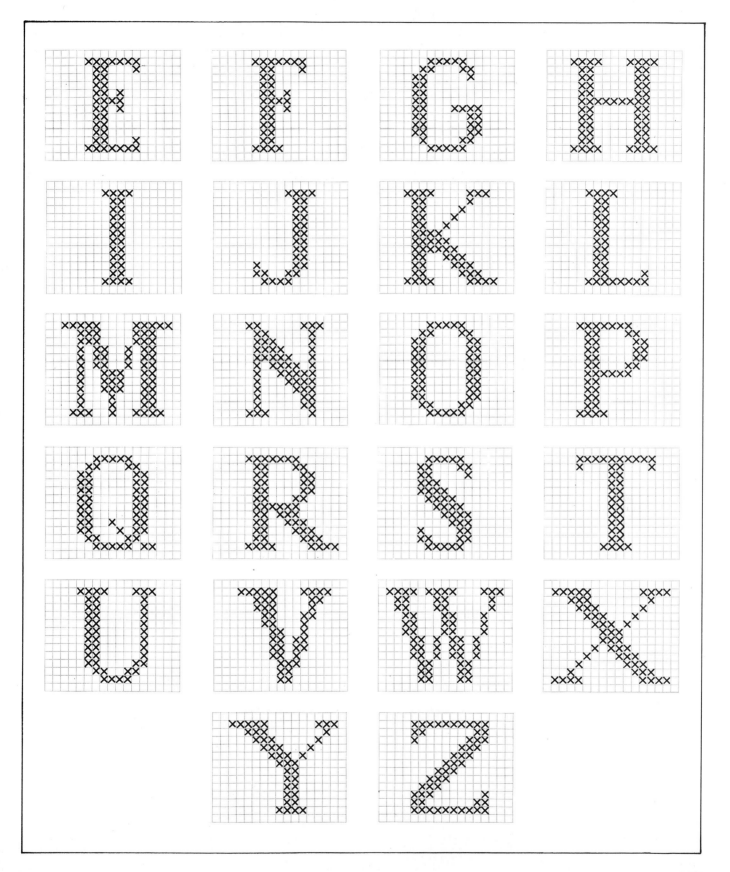

Sweet dreams

This little pillow can be filled with sleep-inducing hops or pot-pourri to help speed your way to dreamland.

Size
13 x 10½in

You will need
6 x 4in rectangle of loosely-woven wool fabric, 18 threads to the inch
Stranded embroidery floss in medium and dark brown
Tapestry needle
24½ x 14½in rectangle of printed fabric
⅜yd of 36in-wide medium-weight batting
3½oz hops (available where beer-making supplies are sold) or potpourri
1⅝yd of brown and beige furnishing insertion braid (with canvas edge), or cording
Sewing thread to match fabric
Sewing thread

To work the embroidery
On the rectangle of wool fabric, embroider "Sweet Dreams" in cross-stitch, following the chart given, using two strands of medium brown stranded embroidery floss.

To make the pillow
On the batting, mark a line 10½in from one short edge. Spread the hops or potpourri evenly over the smaller rectangle below this line. Fold the long end of the batting over the hops and make a second fold to form a double layer of batting beneath the hops. Overcast the ends to enclose the hops. Cut the printed fabric in half to make two rectangles 14½ x 12¼in. Cut out a rectangle in one piece of fabric measuring 3¾ x 1½in. Clip into the corners and press under a ⅜in hem all around the hole you have cut. Center the embroidered panel under the hole in the printed fabric. Sew it in place using running stitch. Using one strand of dark brown floss, work whipstitch into the running stitches.
Press ¾in hems to the wrong side all around both pieces of printed fabric. Baste the braid to the wrong side of one fabric piece. Baste the two fabric pieces together with wrong sides facing and the braid showing between the layers. Work tiny running stitches close to the fold on three sides of the case. Insert the hop-filled batting so that the double layer of batting is next to the underside of the pillowcase. Close with running stitches.

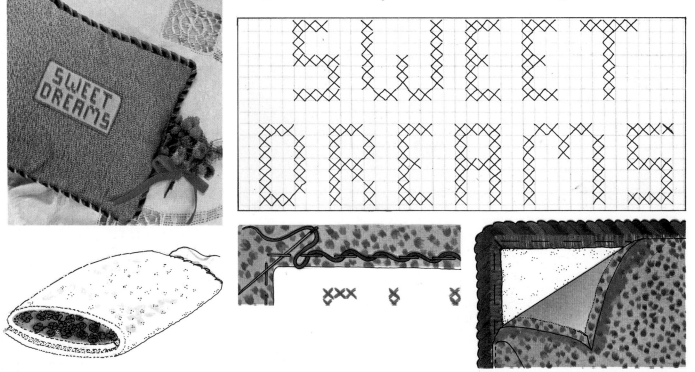

Cherries galore

This colorful cross-stitch design is quick to work and makes a delightful present for an avid reader.

To work the embroidery
Mount linen in hoop. Using two strands of stranded floss and tapestry needle, work six repeats of the cross-stitch motif, beginning and ending with a leaf. Keep the back as neat as possible as the threads will show through on the right side.

To make the bookmark
When the embroidery is complete, draw out two lengthwise threads, two threads away from the edge of the embroidery on each side. Leave eight threads, then pull out two more. Fold the linen so the gaps of drawn threads coincide and baste in place. Cut off excess linen so the two raw edges meet each other at the center back. Baste together securely.
Draw out one horizontal thread about ½in above the embroidery and another ½in below.
Hemstitch along the outside edge of the lengthwise gap from the bottom drawn thread to the top one (see page 39). Repeat on the other side.
Baste the ribbon in place on the back of the bookmark with raw edges folded under to meet the edge of the gap at the top and bottom of the bookmark. Using a crewel needle, slip stitch in place all around, finishing the inner edges of lengthwise gaps and top and bottom edges.
Remove basting and pull out all the loose threads at top and bottom of the bookmark. The double thickness of linen will make a full double fringe.

Size
12 x 3in

You will need
Piece of evenweave linen, 12in square, with 26 threads to 1in
Stranded embroidery floss, one skein each of red and green
Tapestry needle
12in of 1¼in-wide white ribbon
Fine linen lace thread in white
Embroidery hoop
Fine crewel needle

Skills you need
Cross-stitch
Hemstitching

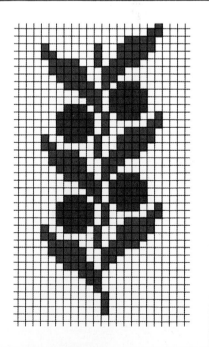

THE
WORLD OF
SAMPLERS

Letters aplenty

Cross-stitch has long been a favorite for embroidered lettering and monograms because it is quick and easy to work. No outline or transfer is needed when an evenweave fabric is used because the fabric threads can be counted to form each letter.

Enlarging the letters
If you want to double the size of the letters, work each stitch over two or more threads.

Reducing the letters
The only way to reduce the size of letters is to use a finer weave fabric.
Monograms—composite intertwined initials—are fun to plan and work. The initials can be arranged so that the base lines are level or diagonal. Plan your monogram on graph paper before you start work so that you can see how the initials link and where they will have stitches in common.

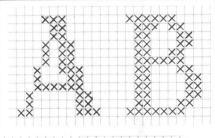

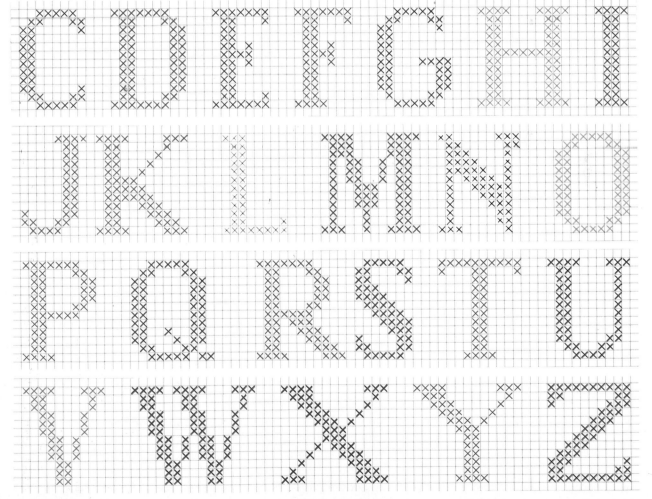

Rainbow sampler

Cross-stitch this bold alphabet sampler and then use your skill to decorate everything from napkins to nightgowns.

Size
10 x 13in

You will need
A rectangle of evenweave linen 3–4in larger all around than the area to be embroidered
Tapestry needle
Stranded embroidery floss in the following colors and quantities:
1–2 skeins in blue, orange, purple, yellow and red (we used 1 skein each for our sampler; if yours will be larger, you may need 2 skeins)
3 skeins in green
Embroidery hoop or frame (optional)

To work the embroidery

Cut the linen to the appropriate size (ours is 16 x 20in).
Mark the center of the linen with a pin.
Count the number of graph squares included in the design from side edge to side edge. Multiply this figure by the number of threads each stitch is to cover (3 in our sampler). Divide this total by 2. Then count this number of threads from the center out to each side of the linen and mark with a pin. These are the side edges of the areas to be embroidered. Following the procedure above, mark the upper and lower edges of the area to be embroidered.
Baste around these edges of the embroidery area following the threads marked. You may also mark the center with a thread.
Using 6 strands of embroidery floss, stitch the outer border first, starting in the center at the top and working out first to one side, then to the other. Then complete the sides and bottom. Complete the inner border, then work the alphabet, flower basket and butterflies.
Turn under the edges all around and press. If it is necessary to press the embroidered area, press face down on a folded towel or soft blanket.

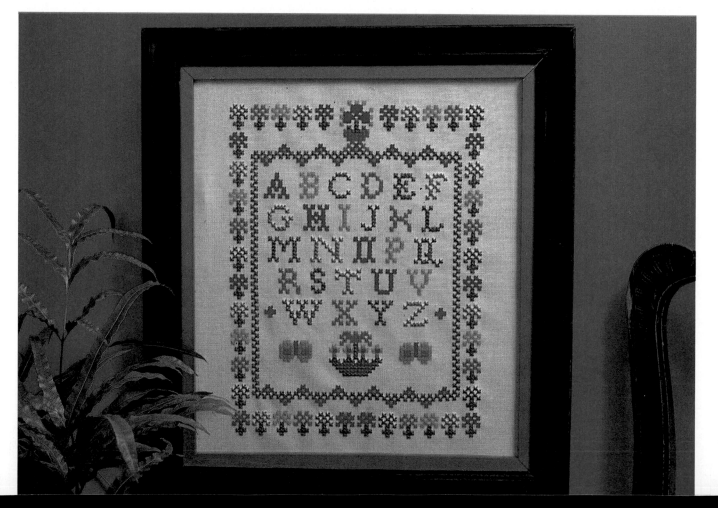

From the garden

This delicious-looking sampler will brighten up the kitchen or breakfast room.

Size
8 x 11in

You will need
⅜yd of 24in-wide evenweave cotton, 18 threads to 1in
Stranded embroidery floss in the following colors and quantities: 1 skein each of light green, medium green, dark green, pink, yellow, blue, brown, black, red-orange
2 skeins of tomato red
Tapestry needle
Mounting board

Skills you need
Cross-stitch
Backstitch

To work the embroidery
Mark the center of the area to be embroidered with a line of basting stitches in both directions.
Using three strands of floss and working over one thread of the fabric, start by working the ladybug. Count 1 stitch down and 6 stitches to the left of the center to find the top right-hand stitch of the ladybug. Use the photograph as a chart to work the sampler. Add your own motifs to personalize it if you wish.
When the sampler has been completed, work the border. Press on the wrong side and lace it (see page 146) to a piece of mounting board. Frame it if you wish.

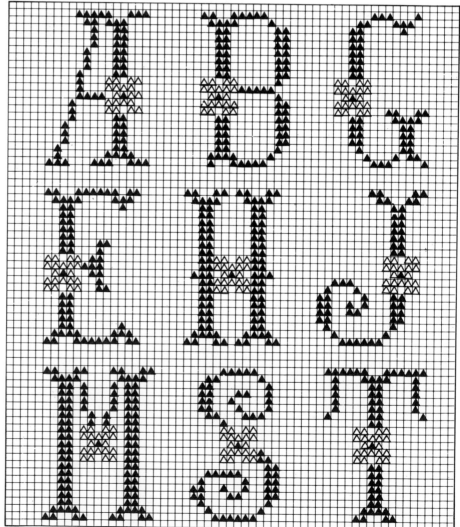

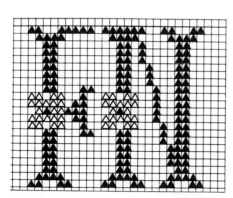

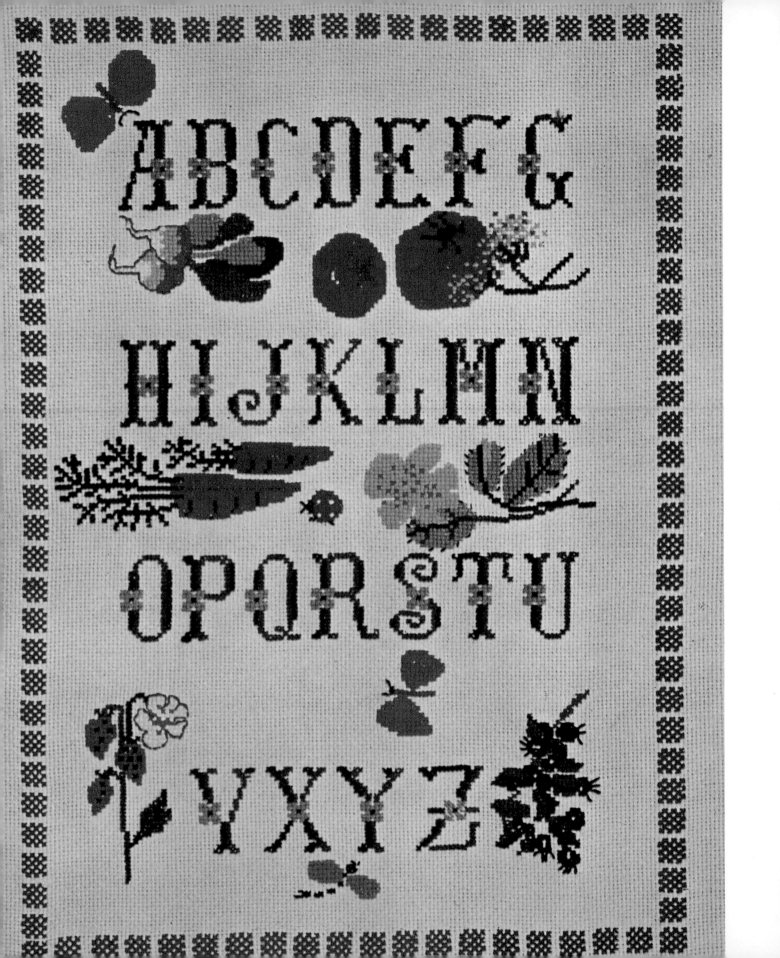

Home sweet home

This attractive Victorian-style sampler has all the charm of times gone by. It can be adapted to suit your own special occasion. Add a personal touch by including your name and the completion date.

To work the embroidery

The best way to work a sampler this size is to mount it on a scroll frame to keep it in shape. It can be worked in the hand without a frame, but will need to be stretched back into shape when it is completed.

Work the sampler in cross-stitch, using two or three strands of floss. Find the center of the canvas and work from the center out, following the chart on page 141. Each square represents one stitch worked over one thread in each direction. Work the design as shown leaving the canvas as the background color. You can, if you wish, fill in the background with cream or beige floss. In this case, work the design first and then fill in the background.

Work one color or a small area of different colors at a time. Do not carry long threads over the back of the canvas between areas of color, because they will show through.

To adapt the sampler

If you want to make an original sampler to commemorate a special event, such as a wedding or the birth of a baby, select a border design to suit the size of your sampler and enhance the alphabet of your choice. Choose the border design and the letters and numbers you will need for the words and

---

Special technique — Mounting canvas in a scroll frame

1. *Cut the canvas or fabric to size, adding an extra 2in all around to the finished dimensions of the sampler. Turn under and baste a ³⁄₈in hem at the top and bottom edges and stitch a piece of 1in-wide webbing or strong tape to the other two sides. Mark the center of the top, the bottom and each side, and baste a line of stitches across in contrasting thread in both directions.*

2. *Match the center top of the material to the center of the webbing on one roller and pin, working from the center out. Overcast, using a strong thread, again from the center out. Repeat with the bottom edge. Fit the arms of the frame into the slots at the end of the rollers and roll any surplus material around the rollers until the canvas is stretched taut.*

3. *Insert the pegs in the arms to secure the frame, making sure the rollers are equally spaced. Thread a chenille needle with carpet thread or strong string, and secure one end around the point where the arm and roller intersect. Lace the webbing to the arm of the frame at 1in intervals to pull the material taut, and tie securely at the other corner.*

date on your sampler and then work out the complete design roughly by tracing the borders, letters and numerals from the chart. When you have got the spacing and proportions right, transfer the whole design to graph paper, using crayons or felt-tip pens or different symbols to indicate the colors. This will make it easier to work the design and count the threads on the fabric when you start to stitch. Alternately, trace each word or line on separate pieces of paper and move them around until you get the position right before transferring the design to graph paper. Mark the center square of your design to help you to position it properly on the fabric.

Borders, which usually consist of a repeat pattern that must fit properly into the corner design, can be difficult to work. It is a good idea to begin with the middle repeat and work out toward each corner.

Or you can make a row of embroidery on the top and bottom edges of the work and eliminate the side edges of the border. It often helps to adjust the distance between the border and the edge of the central design. The spacing and positioning of the central design can also be altered to fit the area within the border.

More design ideas

Letters and numbers can be embroidered in a variety of styles. Use the alphabet to personalize fashion items or objects for the home or add a personal touch to a carefully chosen present by embroidering the initials of a friend. The letters could also be used to make a message for a birthday, wedding or christening.

138

Where the heart is

Size
9 x 8½in

You will need
³⁄8yd of 24in-wide evenweave linen,
28 threads to 1in
1 skein of stranded embroidery floss in
each of the following colors: peach,
light pink, shell pink, dusty pink, rose
pink, red, light blue, violet, mauve, light
purple, medium purple, lilac, deep
purple, apricot, deep green, light
green, yellow-green, yellow, orange
2 skeins of leaf green
Tapestry needle

This lively picture brings a fresh approach to the old-fashioned
sampler. It could be a special birthday greeting, a
housewarming present, or mounted and covered with heatproof
glass, it could be a hot-plate.

To work the embroidery
The charts are planned so that you can use the motifs individually or group
them to make the complete composition. Each element of the design has
its own color coding to provide a permanent reference which you can use
again and again.
Mark the center of the fabric with a line of basting stitches, whether you are
working a single motif or the complete composition. Starting at the center
working outward makes counting the threads easier.
Each square of the chart represents 2 threads of fabric. Work the stitches
using 3 strands of embroidery floss throughout.

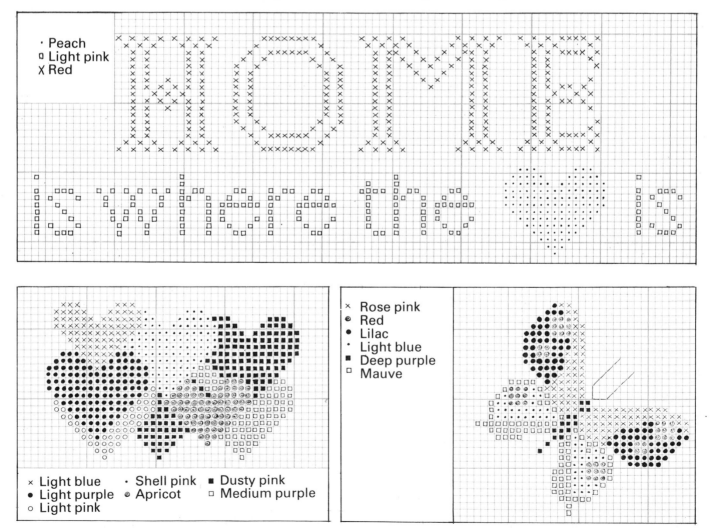

· Peach
▫ Light pink
✗ Red

× Rose pink
◉ Red
● Lilac
· Light blue
■ Deep purple
▫ Mauve

× Light blue   · Shell pink   ■ Dusty pink
● Light purple   ◉ Apricot   ▫ Medium purple
○ Light pink

To finish the sampler
When completed, press the embroidery lightly on the wrong side. If you
are making a picture, see page 146. You can, if you wish, take any
embroidery to an expert for mounting and framing.

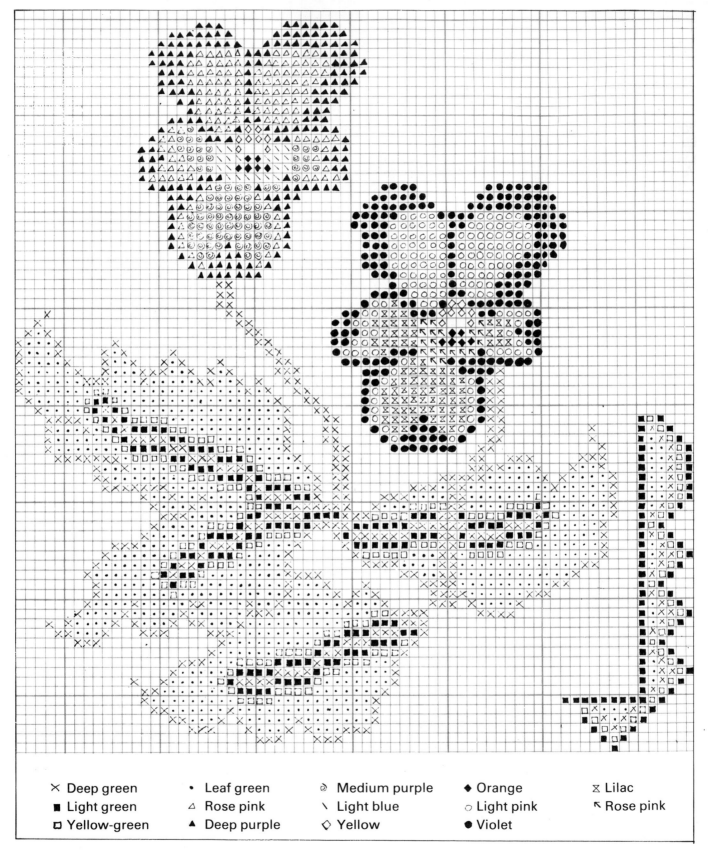

✕ Deep green	• Leaf green	∂ Medium purple	◆ Orange	✕ Lilac
■ Light green	△ Rose pink	\ Light blue	○ Light pink	↖ Rose pink
▱ Yellow-green	▲ Deep purple	◇ Yellow	● Violet	

The best tradition

Work your own sampler in the 20 different stitches that make this sampler a thoroughly enjoyable technical exercise.

Size
36in square

You will need
1yd of 60-in wide evenweave linen, 21 threads to 1in
Stranded embroidery floss in the following colors and quantities:
1 skein each of light blue-gray (a), medium blue-gray (b), dark blue-gray (c), cream (d), medium brown (e), shell pink (f), salmon (g), geranium red (h)
2 skeins each of medium olive green (i), dark olive green (j), tan (k)
3 skeins of dark brown (l)
Tapestry needles in 2 sizes
Mounting board
Button thread

Skills you need
Cross-stitch
Backstitch
Double cross-stitch
Star stitch
Satin stitch
Brick stitch
Honeycomb filling stitch
Coil filling stitch
Four-sided stitch
Swedish darning
Hemstitching
Couching

To work the embroidery

Cut a piece from the fabric to measure 36in square. Mark the center in both directions with a line of basting stitches.

Diagram 1 gives slightly more than half the design with the center indicated by black arrows. Each background square represents 2 threads of fabric.

Diagram 2 shows the Swedish darning and satin stitch tree. Each background line on this diagram represents one thread of the fabric.

Use 6 strands of thread and the larger tapestry needle for Swedish darning, satin stitch and couching. Use 3 strands and the smaller tapestry needle for the rest of the embroidery.

Begin working in the center. Work four-sided stitch filling, 2 threads down and 6 threads to the left of the crossed basting stitches (coded "14" on Diagram 1). Follow Diagram 1 for the main part of the design. Repeat in reverse from the bottom black arrow to complete the second half. Couching is worked horizontally between the satin stitch sections coded C9.

When the embroidery for Diagram 1 has been completed, work Diagram 2 in the position indicated. The hemstitching borders are worked on all four sides of the completed sampler (see page 40).

To finish

Press the completed sampler on the wrong side. For directions for mounting the sampler, see page 146.

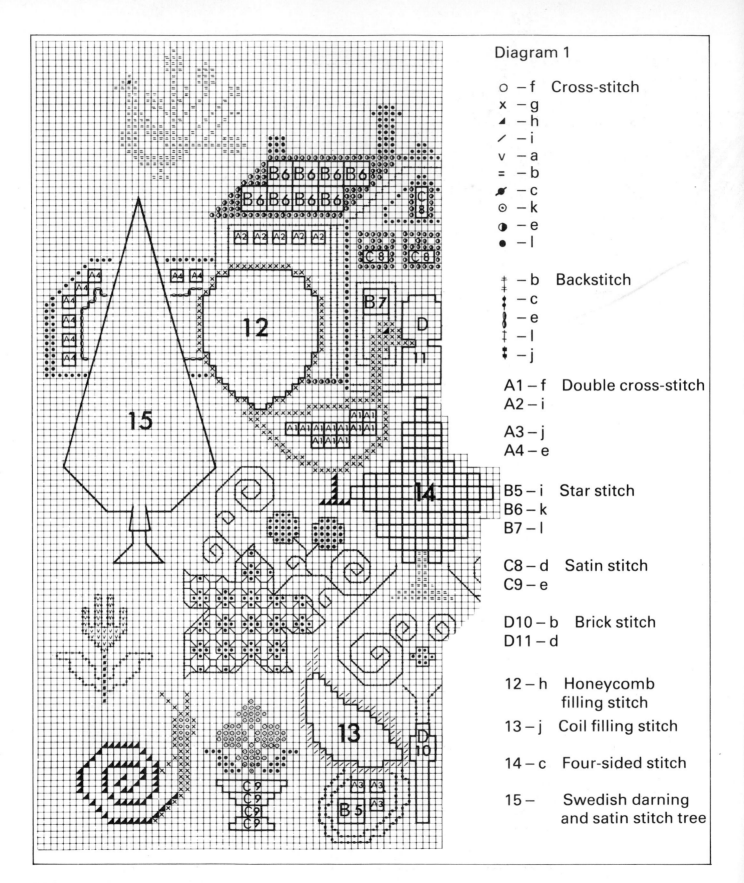

Diagram 1

o – f Cross-stitch
x – g
▲ – h
⁄ – i
v – a
= – b
✘ – c
⊙ – k
◑ – e
● – l

✚ – b Backstitch
✚ – c
✚ – e
✚ – l
✚ – j

A1 – f Double cross-stitch
A2 – i

A3 – j
A4 – e

B5 – i Star stitch
B6 – k
B7 – l

C8 – d Satin stitch
C9 – e

D10 – b Brick stitch
D11 – d

12 – h Honeycomb
         filling stitch

13 – j Coil filling stitch

14 – c Four-sided stitch

15 – Swedish darning
      and satin stitch tree

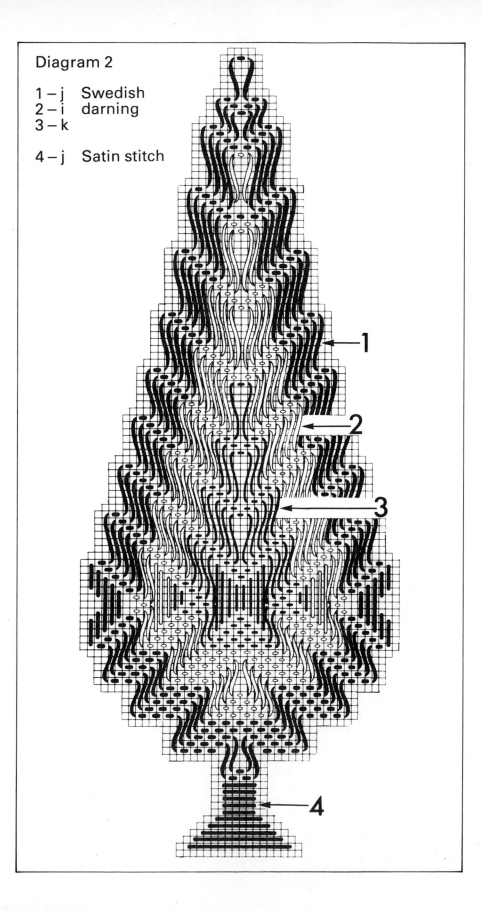

Diagram 2

1 – j   Swedish
2 – i   darning
3 – k

4 – j   Satin stitch

1

2

3

4

Olde-worlde sampler

This delightful country scene depicts birds, beasts and an old English rose border so popular in the traditional samplers of the seventeenth century.

Size
11¼ x 15¼in

You will need
½yd of 60in-wide evenweave linen, 21 threads to 1in
Stranded embroidery floss in the following colors and quantities: 1 skein each of sky blue (a), kingfisher blue (b), turquoise (c), dark tan (d), light brown (e)
2 skeins each of salmon (f), peacock blue (g), light olive (h), dark apricot (i), terracotta (j), dark brown (k), chestnut brown (l)
3 skeins each of leaf green (m) and medium olive (n)
Tapestry needle
Mounting board
Button thread

Skills you need
Cross-stitch
Backstitch

To work the embroidery
Cut the fabric to measure 20 x 24in. Turn the edges under and baste in place to prevent raveling while you work. Mark the center in both directions with a line of colored basting stitches.

The chart shows the complete design, except for the border, which is shown in half repeat. Blank arrows indicate the center, which should coincide with the basting stitches. Work the second half of the border in reverse from from these arrows. Each background square on the diagram represents two threads of fabric counted in both directions.

The whole design is worked in cross-stitch with the exception of the lettering and the fine details on the well, which are worked in backstitch. Both stitches are worked over two threads throughout.

Using four strands of floss throughout, work the embroidery, starting at the center. Follow the color and position key to complete the picture. Work the second half of the border in reverse from the center arrow. Press the embroidery on the wrong side.

Note
The date and slogan can easily be changed using any of the alphabets in this chapter.

To finish
Place the embroidery on the center of a mounting board and secure one side with pins pushed into the edge of the board. Repeat on the other three sides, pulling evenly until the embroidery is taut. Lace the edges across the back from side to side in both directions, as shown below. Use a strong button thread or string for lacing. Remove the pins; the embroidery can be mounted into a picture frame if you wish.

Special technique — Mounting a sampler

Cut the mounting board to the correct size. Center the embroidery on the board and secure it with pins on all sides. Fold the excess fabric back and turn under the raw edges. Lace back and forth with strong thread or string as shown.

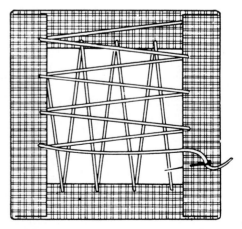

▼ Join arrows ▼

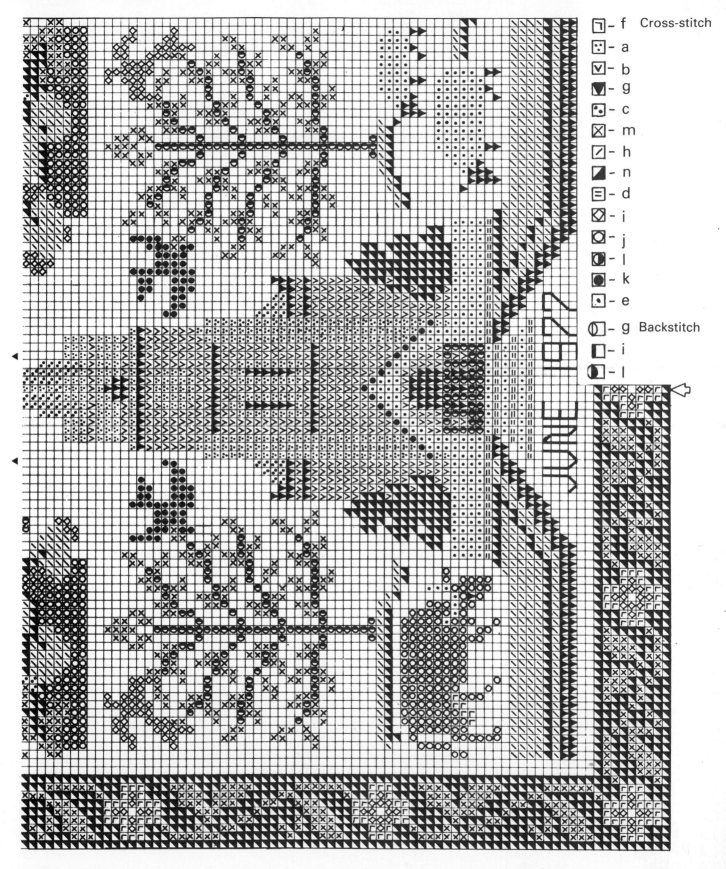

Country sampler

This beautiful sampler is not only an attractive picture, but also has a variety of stitches to test your embroidery skills.

Size
23 x 15in

You will need
¾yd of 59in-wide evenweave fabric, 21 threads to 1in
Stranded embroidery floss in the following colors and quantities:
3 skeins light moss green (a); 2 skeins each cerise (b), peacock blue (c), dark moss green (d), light laurel green (e), dark laurel green (f), parrot green (g), orange (h), cinnamon (i), white (j); 1 skein each cardinal red (k), chestnut brown (l), light gray (m), dark gray (n), black (o)
Tapestry needles in 2 sizes
Scroll frame with 27in tapes
Mounting board
Button thread

Skills you need
Cross-stitch
Satin stitch
Trammed straight gobelin stitch
Backstitch
Tent stitch
Gobelin filling stitch
Straight stitch
Swedish darning

To begin
Cut a piece of fabric 27½ x 23½in. Mark the center of the fabric, both lengthwise and widthwise, with two lines of basting. Mount the fabric in the frame, with short edges on the tapes.
The charts on the following pages give a little more than half the design. Match the two sections together to obtain the complete diagram. The center lines are indicated by blank arrows. When working, match these marked lines with the lines of basting on the fabric.
Each background square on this diagram represents two fabric threads. The numbers in brackets in the key represent the number of threads the stitch is worked over.

To work the embroidery
Begin working at the center of the design, 13 threads down from, and one thread to the right of, the crossed lines of basting, working cross-stitch in dark laurel green (f).
Work the left side of the sampler as given in the two diagrams, omitting the tree and following the diagram and key for the correct colors and stitches.
Instructions for working all the stitches are in the Stitch Library. Use six strands of embroidery floss when working Swedish darning. Use four strands for trammed straight gobelin stitch, tent stitch, satin stitch and straight stitch. Use three strands for cross-stitch and gobelin stitch filling. Use two strands for backstitch.
Use the no. 24 tapestry needle when working with two, three and four strands of floss and the no. 20 tapestry needle when working with six strands.
When working gobelin stitch filling areas over four fabric threads, work the stitches horizontally. When working over two fabric threads, work the stitches vertically.
On the sides of the basket handle, on the front of the main building and on the tree trunk the trammed straight gobelin stitches are worked horizontally. All the other trammed straight gobelin stitch is worked vertically.
The backstitch on the portico is worked on top of the white cross-stitch.
Repeat the design in reverse from the lower blank arrow, omitting the areas already worked.
Continue to work the border section all around the four sides.
To complete the design, work the two trees, following the diagram and key on the left and below. The background lines on this diagram represent the threads of the fabric.
When the embroidery has been completed, press on the wrong side.

To mount the sampler
Place the embroidery over the center of the cardboard. Position it with the right side up and secure it to the board. Fold back the excess fabric and lace both lengthwise and widthwise with strong thread. Remove the pins.

151

152

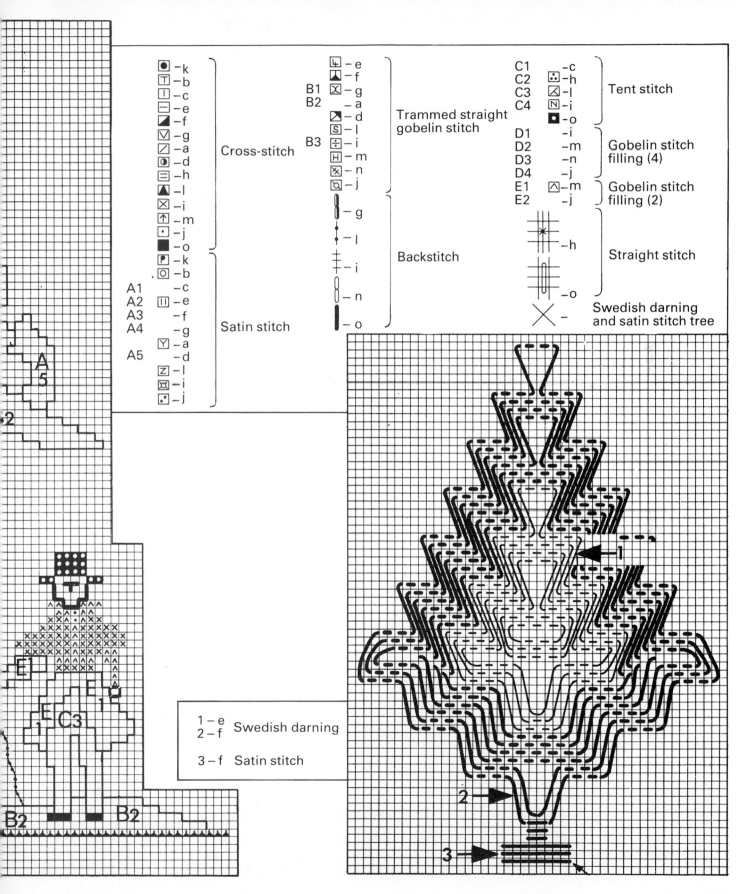

Cross-stitch:
● – k
T – b
I – c
⊟ – e
◺ – f
∨ – g
⧄ – a
◑ – d
⊟ – h
▲ – l
✕ – i
↑ – m
⊡ – j
■ – o

Satin stitch:
A1 P – k
A2 ⊙ – b
A3 – c
A4 Ⅲ – e
A5 – f
– g
Y – a
– d
Z – l
⊠ – i
⊡ – j

Trammed straight gobelin stitch:
B1 ⌐ – e
B2 ▲ – f
⊠ – g
– a
◺ – d
B3 S – l
⊞ – i
H – m
⊠ – n
◨ – j

Backstitch:
– g
– l
– i
– n
– o

Tent stitch:
C1 ⊡ – c
C2 ⊡ – h
C3 ⊠ – l
C4 N – i
● – o

Gobelin stitch filling (4):
D1 – i
D2 – m
D3 – n
D4 – j

Gobelin stitch filling (2):
E1 ◺ – m
E2 – j

Straight stitch:
– h
– o

Swedish darning and satin stitch tree
✕ –

1 – e   Swedish darning
2 – f
3 – f   Satin stitch

153

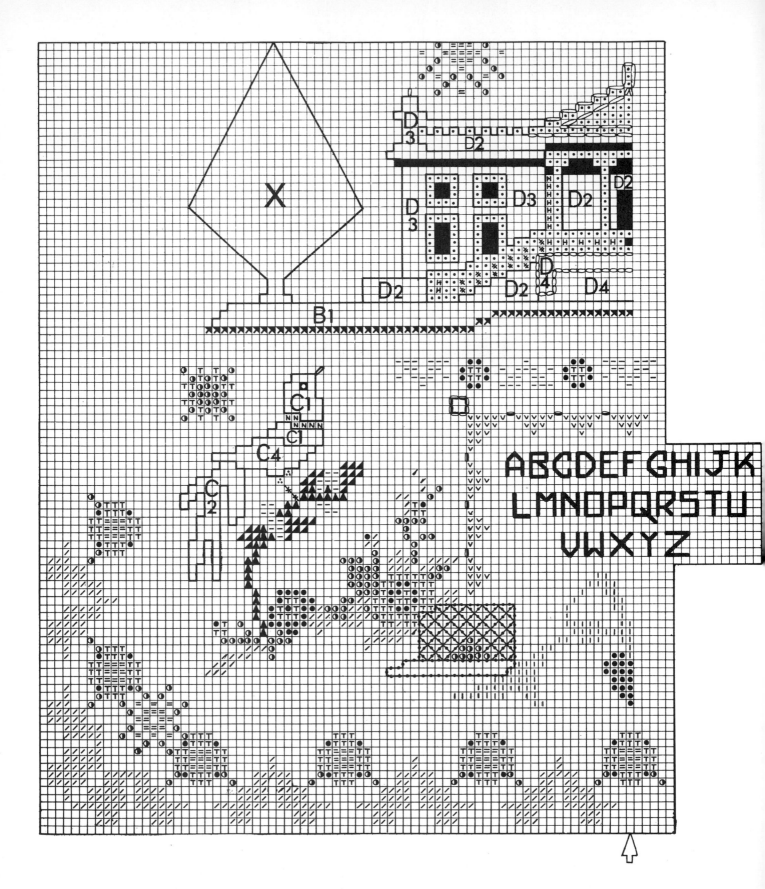

ASSISI
EMBROIDERY

Assisi embroidery originated in Italy in a little Perugian town called by that name in the fifteenth or sixteenth century. The local nuns by tradition made beautiful ecclesiastical linens for their churches using stylized animals, birds and flowers in memory of their patron Saint Francis, or worked geometric patterns taken from mosaics, carvings and ironwork. The embroidery was worked in threads of rust red and black or china blue and navy, which were the traditional colors of the church.

Assisi work looks stunning on all kinds of home furnishings worked either in the original colors or up-dated with strong colors such as green or orange.

Materials

Stranded embroidery floss, matte embroidery cotton, pearl cotton and *coton á broder* are all recommended for Assisi work. For an exotic, modern interpretation use gold metallic thread for the cross-stitch background and either black stranded floss or black metallic thread for the outlines.

Because Assisi embroidery is worked by counting threads, it must be worked on an evenweave fabric, either cotton or linen. Traditionally, natural- or cream-colored fabric is used and is sometimes called Assisi cloth. In general, the threads should be of a similar thickness to the warp and weft threads of the fabric. The finer the weave, the more attractive the design will be.

Method of working

The unique effect of Assisi work is achieved by using two stitches to work the embroidery — Holbein, or double running, stitch for the outlines, and cross-stitch for the background. The motif itself is left showing through the plain unworked background fabric.

All the stitches must be worked over the same number of threads. Work the outlines first and, once they are completed, fill in the cross-stitch background by working the cross-stitches in horizontal lines. The wrong side of the work should be perfectly even and not have long threads carried across the unworked areas of the fabric.

If the outlines follow a diagonal line and it is not possible to make a complete cross-stitch, the spaces can be filled in with a half cross-stitch, but it is better to try to arrange the design so that this is not necessary. If you want to make up or adapt your own design, work it out on graph paper first.

To finish

A plain or hemstitched hem can be used, but traditional Assisi embroidery is finished with an edging of four-sided stitch. Turn the hem under once and baste it. Work a row of four-sided stitch firmly over the edge of the doubled fabric to give a neat, corded edge. The excess fabric is then cut away with very sharp scissors.

Birds and animals, often used in Assisi embroidery, can be reversed or repeated to make charming borders on a variety of items.

Birds and flowers

This traditional tablecloth will cover a cardtable or brighten up a square dining table.

To make the tablecloth
Trim the fabric to make a precise square measuring 46in by cutting along the grain lines. Find the center by folding the fabric in half both horizontally and vertically and basting along the creases with contrasting thread, following the grain. The intersection point marks the center of the tablecloth. Turn under ¼in on all edges and baste down to keep the fabric from raveling while you are working.

The chart gives just over half of one side of the square design in the center of the cloth. Each square represents one stitch worked over three threads of evenweave fabric. The center is indicated by the white arrow, which should coincide with one line of basting. Begin the Holbein stitch outline at the small black arrow 213 threads down from the crossed basting stitches, and follow the pattern as shown on the chart.

Size
45in square

You will need
1⅜yd of 54in-wide evenweave fabric in cream, 30 threads to 1in
Pearl cotton no. 8: 3 skeins China blue, 1 skein black
Tapestry needle
Embroidery hoop

Skills you need
Cross-stitch
Holbein stitch

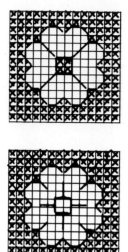

Two simple treatments of the same flower shapes.

The design is repeated as a mirror image on the other half of the first side. Work the remaining three sides to correspond.

Working the outline
Work all the embroidery in a hoop. Embroider the entire outline of the bird and flower design first in Holbein stitch, using black pearl cotton. Work the lines of the pattern inside the motifs, such as the bird's eyes and the flower centers, at the same time as working the outline.

Working the background
When the outline is completed, fill in the background with horizontal lines of cross-stitch, using blue pearl cotton. Work all the stitches with the top stitch facing the same way.

Continue each row as far as it will go and fill in any separate areas later. The back of the cloth should look as good as the front, so the thread should not be carried over any of the unworked motifs.

Where the outline is a diagonal line, use half a cross-stitch only in filling in the background.

Finally, work the inner and outer borders in Holbein and cross-stitch as shown on the chart, using blue pearl cotton.

Finishing
Press the embroidery on the wrong side. Turn under a ¾in hem all around, mitering the corners as shown below, and slip stitch in place. A more decorative hem can be worked by withdrawing one or two threads around the edges of the tablecloth and finishing them with hemstitching (see page 39). Finally, repeat the Holbein and cross-stitch border about 3in from each edge of the tablecloth.

Special technique — Mitering a corner

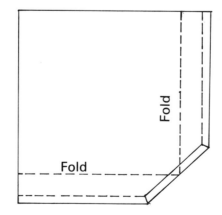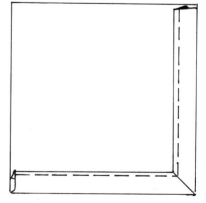

1. *Trim across the corner as shown, leaving ⅛in for turning under. Turn the corner edge under and press.*

2. *Press the edges under ⅛in and turn up the hem. Fit the corners together and slip stitch in place.*

Center

Each square represents
one stitch worked over
three threads of fabric

Work Holbein stitch outlines
in black
Work cross-stitch background
and borders in blue

Design for half of one side

159

Modern myths

This attractive tablerunner is worked in a traditional Assisi color in a design typical of those found in early sixteenth-century pattern books. It would also make a pretty dresser cloth.

Size
18 x 42in

You will need
⅝yd of 54in-wide evenweave linen in ivory
3 skeins of coton à broder in blue
Tapestry needle
Embroidery hoop

Skills you need
Cross-stitch
Holbein stitch
Hemstitching

To make the runner

Find the center of linen by folding it widthwise and lengthwise and mark with a line of basting stitches in a contrasting thread. Then find the width-wise center of each end and mark these points with basting. Center the Assisi design, as shown on the chart, across one end of the tablerunner, using the basting as a guide. The base of the main Assisi design should be approximately 5in from the selvage of the linen.

Work the Holbein stitch outline and fill in the cross-stitch background. Both the Holbein and the cross-stitch should be worked over three threads.

Once the Assisi work is completed on one end, work the Holbein stitch border along the top and bottom of the design. Repeat the small border motif 29 times along both long edges of the tablerunner and then across the other end. Center the Assisi design beneath the border at the end and work as before.

Special technique — Italian hemstitching border

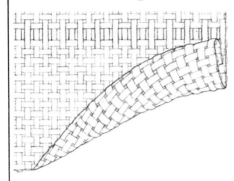 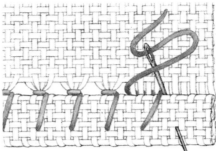 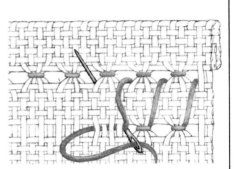

1. *First work Antique hemstitching to hold the hem in place. Withdraw one or two threads 10 to 15 threads from the edge, depending on the weight of your fabric. Roll under the hem to the edge of the drawn threads.*

2. *Work hemstitching from left to right on the wrong side. Pick up four vertical threads, inserting the needle to the right of the threads, and bringing it through to the left. Re-insert the needle and pass it between the hem and the fabric, bringing it out two threads to the right and four threads down. Pull firmly and repeat.*

3. *Work Italian hemstitching from right to left on the right side. Withdraw a single thread five threads from the hemstitching. Bring the needle out to the right side of the hemstitching. Insert it five threads down and encircle four threads to the left. Re-insert it and pass it diagonally upward, bringing it out to the left of the hemstitching, ready for the next stitch.*

To finish

To finish the embroidery with traditional Italian hemstitching, roll a narrow hem and sew in place to produce a neat edge.

The corners of the tablerunner can be decorated with tassels. Pass a length of coton à broder six or eight times through the corner of the Italian hemstitch border and around the left index finger to give a consistent length to the tassel. Wind the thread twice around the top of the tassel between the finger and the edge of the linen to secure it. Fasten off with two or three stitches on the wrong side.

More design ideas
*Peasant-style clothes look very pretty with a border of Assisi embroidery. Work a panel around the hem of a gathered skirt.
Use a single motif to decorate a pocket.*

Cross-stitch

Half cross-stitch

Holbein stitch

Turning the corner

STITCH LIBRARY

All the stitches illustrated in the **Stitch Library** are used in one or more of the projects featured in this book. The **Skills You Need** section included with each project lists the stitches needed for that project.

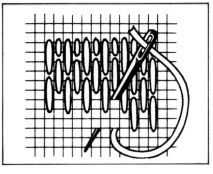

Backstitch for outlining

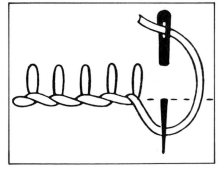

Brick stitch for filling

Buttonhole stitch for outlining and finishing edges

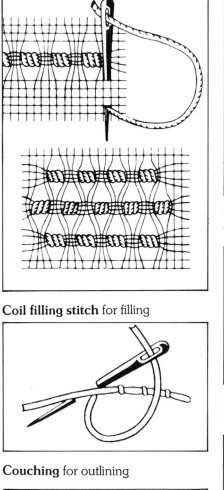

Coil filling stitch for filling

Couching for outlining

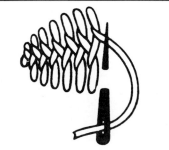

Cretan stitch for filling
Can be worked in a straight line for outlining

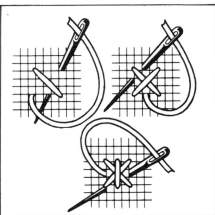

Double cross-stitch for filling or outlining

Eyelet stitch for filling or reinforcing holes

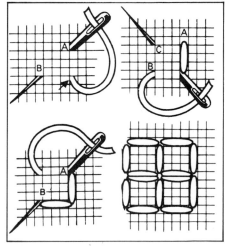

Four-sided stitch for filling

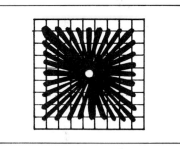

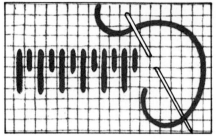

Gobelin stitch (1) for filling
Worked over four threads, then two
threads

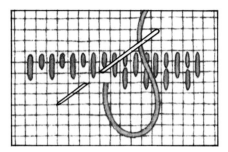

Gobelin stitch (2) for filling
Worked over two threads, then one
thread

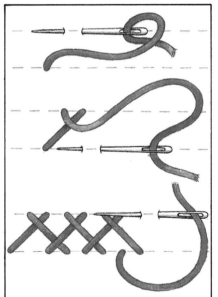
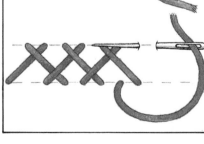
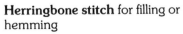

Herringbone stitch for filling or
hemming

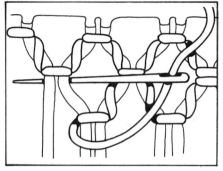

Holbein, or double running, stitch
for outlining

Honeycomb stitch for smocking

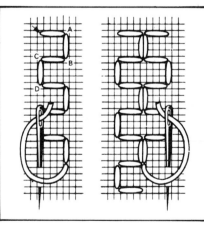

Honeycomb filling stitch for filling

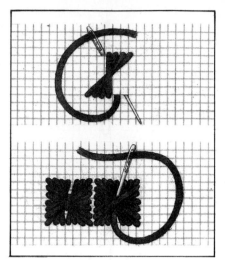

Rhodes stitch for filling

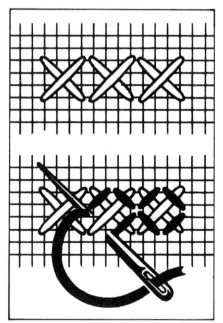

Rice stitch for filling or outlining

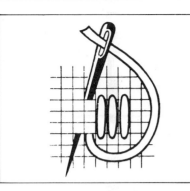

Satin stitch (1) for filling or outlining

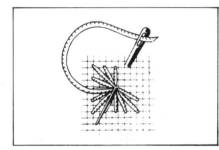

Satin stitch (2) for filling on the diagonal

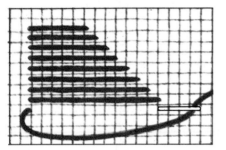

Star stitch for filling or reinforcing holes

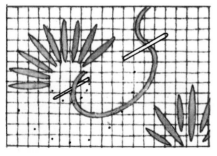

Straight stitch for filling or outlining

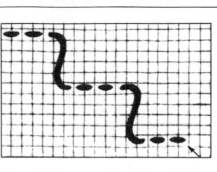

Swedish darning stitch for outlining

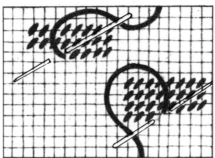

Tent stitch for filling

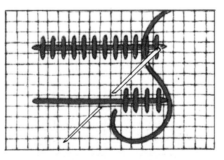

Trammed straight gobelin stitch for outlining or filling

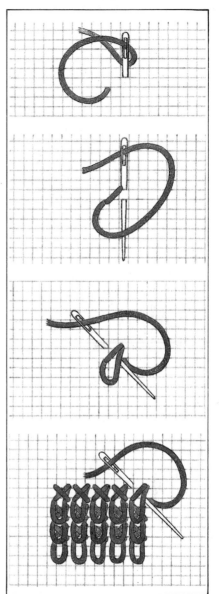

Velvet stitch for filling
Combines loop stitch and cross-stitch

INDEX